The
Singing
Cure

Amanda Lohrey

Rishi
Falmouth, Tasmania, 7215
Australia

ISBN: 978-0-9875938-0-1

Keywords:
Singing, choir, voice, depression, health, spirituality

Cover design and book layout by Michelle Lovi

Amanda Lohrey lives in Tasmania and writes fiction and non-fiction. She has taught politics at the University of Tasmania and Writing and Textual Studies at the University of Technology Sydney, and the University of Queensland. Amanda's award winning novels include, *The Morality of Gentlemen*, *The Reading Group*, *Camille's Bread*, *The Philosopher's Doll* and *Vertigo* plus a collection of short stories, *Reading Madame Bovary*.

Amanda is a regular contributor to *The Monthly* magazine and a former Senior Fellow of the Literature Board of the Australia Council. In November 2012 she received the prestigious 2012 Patrick White Award for literature.

Amanda has a website: www.spiritualstories.net

Contents

Introduction

In 1996 I was invited by the Australian writers Drusilla Modjeska and Robert Dessaix to contribute to a book on the subject of secrets. The book was eventually published in 1997 under the title *Secrets* and what is now *The Singing Cure* appeared under the title, 'The Clear Voice Suddenly Singing'.

At that time I was intrigued by the growth of popularity in *a capella* groups and the resurgence of interest in choral singing and I decided to take the opportunity offered me by Modjeska and Dessaix to research the trend. While scarcely a secret it seemed to me that what underlay this passion for singing was little known or understood in the community. Often it was assumed that it was 'natural' to want to sing but why that activity had the power to bring about a sense of profound physical and psychological well-being was a phenomenon that I felt had yet to receive its share of attention. I set out to interview a number of people I knew for whom singing was as important as breathing and from that beginning I put together this extended essay on one of the fundamental mysteries of our being. We don't need to sing in the way that we need to eat or drink or procreate and yet for many of us singing is one of the most satisfying experiences of our lives. I still recall the woman I sat next to at a dinner party who asked me what I was working on. When I told her, she exclaimed her approval and informed me that every morning she sang for half an hour before breakfast. 'I literally tune myself up for the day,' she said.

Since the original publication I have received many messages from musicians and professional singers to say how pleased they were to discover at last an essay that gave the subject its due. There is, however, a great deal more to be said and each new reader will extend the compass of the essay with his or her own experience. Every year in every country new choirs are formed and new communities of the voice develop. Alone or with others we continue to raise our voices to the sky.

Amanda Lohrey 2013

Part 1

1

Sacred Egoism

I am standing next to Bridie and she is singing too loudly. We are standing in a circle of twenty or so women in the Trinity Church Hall on top of Trinity Hill in Hobart. The hall is old and draughty and some of us are wearing coats. Outside is the city's red-light district, decaying terraces with iron grilles. Across the road is a small park on the steep side of the hill, facing the mountain. Once the Trinity Church graveyard, the park is now a well-known haunt for drug dealing; syringes lie under the park benches and shadowy figures hover in the side alley beneath the autumnal sycamores. And we're inside the Trinity Hall singing, with the door wide open to the cold night.

Soon . . .
Soon . . . death comes creepin in my room
Soon . . .
Soon . . . death comes creepin in my room
Hush . . .
Hush . . . somebody's callin my name

At least, some of the time we sing. For much of the time, however, we vocalise. This means we stand in a circle and improvise on a note, pitching our voices to the centre of the circle into a column of sound. Is this sound column purely metaphorical? It depends on where you're standing. If you are at the centre of the circle with your eyes shut you feel the sound vibrating across your shoulders and chest, the base of your neck begins to tingle and you begin to sway a little, forward and back, and you become aware of someone quietly moving in behind you in case you fall.

But tonight I'm not in the middle, tonight I'm on the rim of the circle and I'm standing next to Bridie and she is singing too loud, that is, her strong, pure soprano voice is soaring above my hoarse insipid contralto. She is purposeful and at ease; she is a soprano and she knows it. As usual, I am confused. I have two voices and I don't know which one to sing with. Why can't I just open my mouth and let my voice fall out? Like Bridie. Instead, I have to think about it. There is my chest or throat voice that is like my talking voice; deep and conversational with a slightly abrasive edge and good volume. But the problem with this voice is that after a while I get a sore throat. I rely too much on the muscles of the neck, forget to breathe in the right places, close off the base of the throat and suffer. Then I switch to my head voice, my higher and lighter and more effortless voice, but with no top notes. Above a certain range the voice disappears, cuts out altogether or gives a light high-pitched squeak. My resonating chambers in 'the mask' (nose, forehead, sinuses) fail me. And I don't like the sound of myself. This is a prim little folk singing voice; plaintive. I sound like a timid female. I like my resonant chest and throat voice, the strong one, but that's the voice that tires. Head or chest? Throat or mask?

Bridie is soaring. She is up there in the rafters, she is wafting across to the furthest corners of the hall, past the basketball hoops and above the chequered stage curtain. Next Tuesday evening I will stand next to someone else, someone who is, well, *less of a natural*. No one who knew me would ever accuse me of being natural. If I were a *natural* would I sit behind a computer day after day shuffling words around on the page, devising the various masks of fiction to hide behind? No, I wouldn't. And I surprise myself by being here. I have been coming to this group for nine weeks and for the first three sessions I hated it. Now I am becoming addicted. But I don't know why I'm addicted, or what it is that I'm addicted to.

When the session is over we troop out into the frosty night air and I wait for Beatrice to unlock her car and give me a lift home. Driving down the precipitous Glebe hill, past the many mansions of Victorian gothic we begin to talk about why it is that we come, especially on bitter nights like this, and I recall an encounter in mid-air over the Pacific.

2

The Secret Self

It is August 1986 and I am flying to the USA to spend a year in Berkeley. My husband is already there, looking for a house. My two-year-old daughter and I are on our way. In the long dim cocoon that is the cabin of a 747 cruising at night I croon some lullabies to my daughter, at that moment stretched out across two seats, her head in my lap. Beside me, a handsome middle-aged man dozes fitfully. As the last of my muted lullabies trails off he opens one eye and says: 'Do you do requests?'

'Not here,' I murmur.

'In that case I'll just have to count more sheep.' Before long he too appears to be asleep, his head lolling to one side, his dark beard grazing my shoulder.

In the morning we exchange pleasantries over our plastic breakfast trays. He tells me his name is Aaron and he is a professor of psychology at Stanford University where he is doing research into the nature of the work people do and how it correlates with their sense of self. What were their ambitions when they were sixteen? Are they doing at forty what they'd planned or hoped to do in their youth? And what do they see themselves doing in their ideal or fantasy life? Then he tells me the surprise of his findings so far. 'Everybody wants to be a singer,' he says. 'Not a baseball player, not even a movie actor, but a singer. On stage at The Met, headlining at Vegas – if the genie with the lamp appeared tomorrow, that's what they'd ask for.'

Somehow this doesn't surprise me, although I can't say why. Had he, I ask, arrived at an explanation?

No, he says, he and his team haven't got to the follow-up but he is looking forward to interviewing a sample of respondents to his survey and 'coming up with some answers'.

He is of course exaggerating, as one does to frame a conversation point. What he has found is not that *everyone* wants to be a singer but that a surprisingly high number of respondents have given this as their secret ambition in life. And why, he asks, do I think this might be?

I wonder if it isn't obvious? Doesn't everyone want to be noticed, and admired?

Yes, he says, but why singing? There are other ways of seeking the limelight.

3

I first fell in love with unaccompanied singing in the pubs of Norfolk and East Anglia. It was the seventies and I was studying at Cambridge and living in a small village called Waterbeach in which there was no water and no beach because Cromwell had long ago drained the fens. On Saturday nights my boyfriend and I would often drive out into those mysterious fenlands with their endless dark horizon and spend the evening in one of the dour village pubs. I was intrigued by their character, the way in which the public bar was like an extension of someone's living-room and the patrons on a Saturday night ranged from small children with dummies in their mouths to old men who could barely stagger in on a stick. And quite often on these evenings several among the drinkers would sing, solo and unaccompanied. 'C'mon, Bert. Give us a chorus of "Black Velvet Band".' Bert was quite likely in his sixties, short and wiry and wearing a cloth cap and if he were in the mood he'd rise from his table, wait a moment for a respectful silence to fall and give us the full version in a quavering voice that was quite hypnotic in effect. Why I was entranced by these turns I can't say. As I got to know the various pubs I became aware of how the singing for the night would reflect the mood of the community. Feuds, ill fortune, an impending election, anything could and did influence the tenor of the evening; who sang what, who stolidly refused to oblige; who turned her back on the singer of the moment.

I was reminded of this many years later when I went to see Terence Davies' lyrical cinematic portrait of working-class community, *Distant Voices, Still Lives*. Some of the movie's most luminous scenes take place in the local pub where Davies lovingly captures the importance of community singing in the life of his family. Singing in the pub is one of the few times the family is free of physical and emotional violence. This is its moment of peace, of expressing unconditional love, of being free from resentment and recrimination, from the burdens of history or anxieties about the future; of being, simply and for the moment, free. It resonated with times in my own childhood when some tribal event — an anniversary, a wedding reception — would be transported on to another plane by an outbreak of song. I remember still how the faces of the adults would suddenly soften, the expression in their eyes change.

Bert was a different thing altogether. To strangers like us he was the resonance of the landscape itself. Though I have several photographs taken at that time, none can evoke the quality of the fens like the aural memory of Bert's voice and the merest phrase from his song, its strange link to my own origins. '*It's over the dark and blue ocean/Far away to Van Diemen's Land*'. A callow twenty-year-old, I became aware for the first time how much the singer reveals of himself, how undefended an act of self that singing can be, how impossible it is to fake almost anything. Nothing to hide behind, not even an old piano. This is what gives the amateur his grip on our attention; the sense of him walking a tightrope, that anything could happen. Even a mediocre professional has the assured mask of training and technique. In professionals, in all trained singers, the voice is more separated out from the person, almost an entity in itself, something you can insure in its own right. Advanced technique can mask rather than reveal the self. When an amateur sings he seems to offer up his whole body; just the pattern of his breathing can tell you so much; where he looks, what he does with his hands.

4

Another dark space. This time I'm sitting in Hobart's old Theatre Royal with velvet seats and ornate boxes and on the gilded ceiling a circle of portraits, of Handel, Bach and Mozart framing an extravagant chandelier. It's the annual eisteddfod and I've come to watch someone I know sing. That someone is a friend whom I'll call Caroline, now warming up in a backstage dressing-room before coming on to perform two songs from the Schumann song cycle, *Frauenliebe und-leben*, 'A Woman's Love and Life'.

I've known Caroline since the day she was born. Once a pretty, bright-eyed child with flaming red hair, in adolescence she had become stooped and round-shouldered, hunched almost, and some muffling blanket of self-consciousness had descended on her. Often praised as a 'responsible' girl she seemed, as she grew older, to carry the weight of the world on her shoulders. In her late twenties she was treated, on and off, with anti-depressants. At the age of thirty-two she and her husband divorced and she was awarded sole custody of her two small boys. On her thirty-third birthday, out of the blue, her mother suggested she take singing lessons.

I had recently returned to Hobart to live and immediately observed a change in her; she stood up straight and the fire had come back into her eyes. Often over coffee she would talk about her class and her teacher, a woman called

Helen to whom she told everything about herself.

'When I sing it makes me feel relaxed. And it makes me feel important. It's partly to do with breathing, I think. At the end of the lesson I feel high, clear and calm. Not like I used to feel. I used to feel stuck. Now I feel I've broken through.'

Broken through to what?

'It's hard to describe. I feel like I'm in another zone.'

When she was at school, she said, she was told not to sing in the choir, just to stand and mouth the words because her voice wasn't good enough and it 'spoiled the sound'. The rebuff stayed with her; she felt as if her voice had been confiscated, like a piece of flamboyant jewellery that violated the uniform code. For the rest of her school days she didn't even sing in the shower.

'I went along with something I should have rebelled against. I should either have insisted on singing out in the choir or refused to participate at all. Instead of that I stood in the back row and mouthed the words, every year until I left school. Can you believe that?'

Yes, I could believe it. From other stories I had been told, it wasn't all that uncommon an experience. In fact I've heard this story, or some version of it so many times over the years that I've come to think of it almost as a kind of urban myth, internalised. And one of the most memorable accounts comes from, of all people, Tito Gobbi who recalls the following episode in his autobiography *My Life* (1979). 'At one of our rehearsals (for an end-of-term performance) our teacher, Maestro Bevilacqua, started going round the class muttering to himself. Finally he stopped in front of me and exclaimed: "You're the culprit! You're shouting like a mad dog – it's terrible. You keep silent. But as we don't want [anyone] to know you are not singing, simply open and shut your mouth and pretend to sing.'"

In the year following her first lesson, said Caroline, it began to feel as if she were undergoing a transformation. She had gone along to her first appointment with some nervousness, expecting to be asked to sing. Instead, her singing teacher asked her to move around the room, making sounds.

What sort of sounds?

'Any sounds I liked. Oooohhh and aaaahhh, mostly.' After a few minutes of a kind of crooning she began to cry. 'I felt as if my jaw was locked, and that it had been locked for years. And then I felt it open. It was a weird sensation.

'I had, then, what we, Helen and I, call my "little girl voice". You know, that high piping voice. You know how when you're nervous your voice goes up? Well, mine was up all the time. I was too scared to let the little girl voice go. But somehow, through doing all the exercises, and the scales, and learning to stand differently, hold my head differently, breathe differently . . . Helen used to tell me things, about technique and so on, and after a while I realised that what she was really telling me was that it was okay to grow up. And from that moment on my voice began to change, it got a deeper tone. And it got louder. Much louder. Now my voice just seems to get bigger and bigger.' She laughed, half apologetically. 'Some days it's so big it scares me.'

And I'm thinking: how come my voice isn't big enough to scare me? What am I missing?

Listening to Caroline I think I recognise something both remote and yet familiar, some faint echo of the ineffable, something maybe to do with awe. *Awe*. It's an old-fashioned word, a biblical word, a mixture of fear and reverence, a sense of benign mystery, a glimpse of the terror of the sublime. On a more prosaic level I also recognise something else, something my own daughter is alerting me to – the difficulty of making the transition from girlhood to womanhood. This is an experience that can take you two ways, along either the dissenting path or the compliant one. Much of the literature about adolescence focuses on the 'difficult' girl, the rebellious one who gets into sex and drugs, precipitates an emotional storm in the house and clears out at the age of fifteen. But then there are those other girls. In the presence of parents, in deference to their love and their idealisation of childhood – or sometimes, even, in sublimated recoil from maternal envy – these daughters are inhibited. Their secret selves have been camouflaged (stooping shoulders, piping voices) for so long that they feel self-conscious – foolish and absurd even – when they perform. For what is performance but a sudden flourishing of the bold and ambitious self, the hungry ego, a ruthless eros. This, I think, explains the phenomenon of why, contrary to the sentimental view, many young performers are more confident performing when their parents are *not* there. And yet in order to make the most of their talent they need some nurturing figure, and if not the parent then someone else.

For Caroline that someone else appeared to be her singing teacher, Helen, a woman whom she frequently cited in conversation, chapter and verse – 'Helen says … Helen suggested' – and who seemed to figure in her landscape not so much as a second mother but as a first muse. I told her this.

'What does the muse do again? Remind me.'

'Opens the throat and enables you to speak. It's a Greek myth. The gods created the world and then found they had no one to sing their praises so they created the Muse. The Greeks believed the existence of things was not complete unless there was a voice to express it.'

'I thought only poets had a muse.'

'Anyone can have one.'

It was somewhere around the time of this exchange that I told Caroline that I thought I would like to write something about why people sing. It wasn't only her own enthusiasm that had aroused my interest and she was not the first of my friends and acquaintances to take up singing. I knew a number of people in Sydney who, since the late eighties, had joined *a cappella* groups or community choirs and some who had arranged to take private lessons, not with any view to pursuing a career but simply for the sake of it. Everyone seemed to know someone who was 'into it' and inevitably the boom in new wave singing groups had begun to attract the attention of the media. Clearly something was afoot in the *Zeitgeist*, something Stephen Schafer, then Musical Director of the Sydney Gay and Lesbian Choir described as 'a new renaissance, a new generation of singers'. I had just completed a novel which examined some of the more idiosyncratic ways in which troubled individuals go about getting themselves into a state of grace and it now occurred to me that singing might be one of them. I rang Helen, Caroline's singing teacher. Could we meet, and could I put to her the simplest of questions (Aaron's question on the plane to Berkeley)? Why do people sing?

5

Helen Todd's studio is a pale blue room at the back of an historic sandstone cottage on the northern edge of the city. On entering the first thing I notice is an enormous Japanese fan over the empty fireplace and a Korg keyboard on a black iron stand. Against one wall is a large desk with many books and papers and a ceramic oil-burner that gives off a hazy scent of cedarwood. Next to the desk is a huge mirror that hangs from floor to ceiling. In the early lessons, Caroline told me, that mirror is disconcerting. To see all of yourself looking back at you in a strange room can be confronting.

Helen is seated at her desk. She is a woman in her forties, slim with blonde hair to just below her shoulders. Perhaps because I know her to have trained as an opera singer I am struck by her resemblance to a more svelte and romantic version of a Wagnerian heroine. During our conversation she will sing to me in order to demonstrate a point and in a few days' time I will hear her sing in recital. She has a strong soprano voice with warm, dark tones and a sexual charisma that is attractive to both men and women.

At this, our first meeting, I begin by reciting Aaron's research findings. I tell her that when I ask people like Caroline why they sing they find it difficult to give me an answer. Helen frowns. 'I suppose they would find it difficult to answer that,' she says. 'You might as well ask them why they breathe.'

Why then, I ask, did she sing?

'When I was a child, if I didn't sing I'd feel desperate. I just had to do it. But each person will give you a different answer. Perhaps you need to ask more people.'

'Supposing,' I say, 'I were to offer myself as a student. What then? How should I go about preparing my audition?'

'You wouldn't,' she says, with quiet emphasis. 'I don't audition.'

'Never?'

'No. If you can talk you can sing. That's the point I start from. It's the *desire* to sing that matters, at least at the beginning.'

Well, then, how would she describe her method?

'I don't have a strict method. My method is constantly changing but the essence of it is the Italian method, *bel canto*, beautiful sound. I do use some of the Melba method, her exercises and vocalises, but her great words of wisdom are in her simple advice.' She takes up a book from her desk. 'See, here. Here on page one, right at the top: *In order to sing well it is necessary to sing easily. Melba's first law, if you like. But how many students are prepared to accept that statement? Very few. They smile and say, it may be easy for you but it's not for me.*' She closes the book and hands it to me. 'That,' she says, 'is when I talk to my students about poise. Poise is critical in singing. When we're poised we're balanced, and when we're balanced we sing easily. When we're tight and restricted, we sing hard. I wince when a student says, Oh, I'm trying so hard. Don't try hard, I say, try gently.'

Take me, I say, through the first lesson.

'First, you have to hear the sound you would like to make, in your head, and then you make that sound. And that assumes that you are motivated, you are some way along the path of changing from being self-conscious to being conscious of self. Self-consciousness is crippling and you have to get rid of it.'

How?

'Simple, you work with the body. You don't stand rigid and statuesque, that's the old stance, the one I was taught. You learn to loosen up so there's a sense of stretching to the heavens as you sing rather than locking your body.

'I might begin with this exercise. I'll ask you to call out – in the studio, at a sports oval, at the beach. "HEY!" (Yes, sorry to startle you.) The point is to make people realise that when there's an alarm, when there's something urgent, you will automatically breathe well and then you make a big sound which is absolutely on top of the breath. So singing is no different. HEYYYY! It's out! So what we're really doing, very quickly – and I usually do this in the first lesson – is getting people to call something out, and usually we stand on our toes and imagine that we're calling out to Mt Nelson. Some people find this difficult. Good children are seen and not heard, a lady is never loud and so on. Once they've done that – shouted HEY! – then straight away I must get them to sing, without any further talking, because that's a new imprint.

'There's a critical question in singing, as in life. Who judges me? Whom do I *allow* to judge me? This is a big issue for us, isn't it? *We* decide who judges us, *we* appoint other people our judges. So I get them to shout. And in shouting, learning to make a big sound naturally, they're usually becoming so engrossed in what they're achieving they're not giving themselves time to judge. I often talk to the student about who's judged them in the past – you have to be very careful about this – and inevitably they come back to saying: I'm always judging myself, I need to judge myself before I let anyone else judge me. So we go through that, and there are a number of stories I've got, and little rituals and games.'

We talk about self-consciousness and inhibition. 'Inhibition,' says Helen, 'is partly an Anglo-Saxon thing. I suspect it happens a lot less in, say, Italy where everyone's expected to carry a tune. And I also think it's something to do with our religious background, the rigidity of the worship, the denial of the senses. Formal, dour. A lot of the people who are working with singing have got those church connections. They're not interested in sensual sound, in full romantic sound, they're interested in what we used to call the sexless, pure sound. And so we're encouraged to make that sexless, pure, piping soprano sound. I've got a bit of a thing about this sexless sound. They feel this is the spiritual sound. I can't go along with that.

'When Caroline came to me and sang it was just beautiful, and pretty, and she hardly breathed in two minutes. I mean, enormous restraint. But I had to ask, where's the warmth? Where's the woman? You have to help them say goodbye to their little girl voices. There are women of fifty still carrying these around.'

How do you develop this warmer voice inside?

'Vibrato. The vibrato appears when it's ready, when the tension drops away. You make long swooping and humming sounds and you start to get a tremendous buzziness or vibration in your voice, and hopefully the larynx is not caught right up and you'll notice that when you go Eeeeeeeeeeeh it's not tight and screechy any more, there is a warmth in your voice. It's to do with trusting yourself, deep down. It's all about having the guts to open your mouth and just let out what's there to be let out, at the given time. So once you get the mental set right you work on this other stuff, the exercises, the vocalises, the technical side. Singing is not just letting it all out. You have to emote, but emote with control.

'Of course, some people come to me for therapeutic reasons above all else. I see people come in who've been stifled, people who talk through their teeth and who can barely get their mouth open. They come in and they tell me their story. There are hundreds of stories, every person has their story. So they come in, they express this, they get here despite their fear, and off we go.'

6

On my first visit to the eisteddfod to hear Caroline I turn up on the wrong day. Late, I fumble my way in the dark theatre, down awkward wooden steps to the front stalls. Once seated I peer at my programme and discover my mistake, but by this time I am beginning to find the spectacle on stage so intriguing that I decide to stay. A young girl, no more than ten and dressed in top hat, white tie and tails is tap-dancing and flourishing a cane. An androgyne Fred Astaire, shuffling in the spotlight, "Puttin' on the Ritz".

It's the children's song-and-dance categories and according to my programme we are up to the Under Elevens. Watching these children perform (they are almost all girls) I become aware of the ways in which the performing child is there not merely to please her teacher, and her mother, but more importantly to act out a repertoire of possible selves. Eliza Doolittle . . . Madonna . . . some long forgotten vaudeville comic . . . Liza Minelli ("New York, New York"), anyone, in fact, you want to be. Absurdly fat girls do ballet solos; self assured little stage brats point their toes, throw up their arms and belt out a tune off key. And the best thing is, at this age no one expects you to be able either to sing or to dance. Or even to look the part. Just to hold your nerve.

As the afternoon sings and dances by I feel as if the history of a musical culture is being laid out for me, endless quotations from and quaint embodiments of a living past. A group of adolescent girls revive Lancashire music hall in the 1930s with a rendition of the George Formby classic, "When I'm Cleaning Windows". Dressed in football socks, shorts and builders labourers' T-shirts they cart a ladder about the stage, strutting through a series of exaggerated male gestures, gawping and leering and sticking their thumbs up at their bemused audience. A chorus line of eight tots, four of them Chinese, step out with precision drilling in transparent yellow raincoats and umbrellas and sing and tap-dance their way through "Singin' in the Rain". And this is just one afternoon, one genre of performance. If you hang around any eisteddfod for long enough you'll hear German lieder, 42nd Street, Banjo Paterson, English art song, Jim Morrison, Mozart, Tommy Dorsey, negro spirituals, Cole Porter, Techno, Acid Jazz and many, many renditions of Andrew Lloyd Webber.

Far from being stifled, many of these small girls seem to have been launched into a precocious maturity. Of a kind. It's true that some children are stifled, but there are others who are over-coached. They sing and dance in a lighted space, the lights go out and then what? I recall a piano teacher who had been a child prodigy telling me how her mother entered her into serious competition from the age of five and how, if she failed to win every section she entered, Mother wouldn't speak to her for days. She was pushed onto a treadmill and the performance space became a place of terror.

It reminds me of Alice Miller's idea of the true self and the false self. The false self is a compliant self, the self that an over-directive mother or father wants the child to be so that the child may enact the parent's own thwarted narcissistic needs. The so-called true self can only emerge if the parent acts as a supportive (open and flexible) nurturer who 'mirrors' the natural narcissistic impulses of the child, including aggression, in a way that expresses unconditional love. Since none of us has perfect parents, all of us are left with a carapace of false self that at some moment, like a dead skin, demands to be shed. What this means at any particular age will depend perhaps on whether we were stifled or overcoached. For the stifled, the voice of the true self has to find a way of speaking out and being heard, and it occurs to me that singing might be one of those ways.

It also occurs to me that there must be more to it than that.

7

Caroline comes second in her section at the eisteddfod, a remarkable result, much better than she or anyone else expected. Afterwards I offer to take her to supper. She is worried about the babysitter but she also knows she is too high even to consider going to bed. She rings home, says she'll be late but not too late and we adjourn to a hotel next to the theatre. There, in celebratory mood, we order a couple of absurd cocktails and try to shut out the miked-up sound of the singer in the piano bar behind us. I want to ask Caroline about her ambition to sing in the eisteddfod. I know she has no desire to be a professional singer, so why compete?

'It breaks down a barrier,' she says. 'It's not so much the competing but the singing in front of an audience. Once you've sung in front of people you feel you can do anything.'

What about making a speech in front of an audience, or acting?

'Not the same.'

Why not?

'I don't know. Can't explain. All I know is that you don't have a sense of anything but the moment. There's no past, there's no present. I mean, it's almost like a revelation. Just everything being perfect and right and proper and in its place. The thing's there as a whole. It's ecstasy.'

Ecstasy? I raise my eyebrows.

'Yes, ecstasy.'

So you sing to get high?

'Yeah, I sing to get high. I know about the physiology of endorphins, and the need to get a hit probably about once a week. And I know I can rely on singing to give me that. I could smoke dope instead but it doesn't work for me. When I'm down, dope only makes me feel worse. Singing, you might say, is my drug of choice. And the beauty of having lessons is that after a while you start to get a . . . well, a stretch. At first you're thrilled just to be able to open your mouth and get a good sound out but then you want more, you want to develop. It's a stretch, you're not just repeating the same thing over and over again. You feel like you're progressing. Sometimes I think it's better than sex. With sex I never feel I'm progressing.'

8

Masterclass

On the following Sunday afternoon I find myself sitting in the recital hall of the Conservatorium of Music. I have come to observe a visiting maestro tutor a class of promising students.

The hall is a steeply rising auditorium with walls of grey concrete block, grey carpet and dark green seats; as blank and characterless a space as all the other institutional auditoria of low-grade modernism. On the front wall, behind the performance space, is a pale blue curtain of thin silk. The space itself is a glossy floor of polished boards on which stands a black grand piano. Out of the corner of my eye I can see Helen Todd sitting two tiers above me, watching the stage intently and waiting for the first of her students to appear.

The atmosphere here is quite different from the preceding Wednesday evening. The eisteddfod had been a kind of festive free-for-all with a slightly lurid and be-sequinned quality. The masterclass is a much more rarefied and, in a sense, poignant space. It's the space of possibility, of true promise, where the young singer is poised between the private devotions of the amateur and the public acclaim of the professional. The master, Ron Maconaghie, is a distinguished former baritone with Opera Australia, now in his sixties. He is a short, broadly proportioned man who could be your local bank manager with glasses and receding brown hair, avuncular and relaxed in grey trousers and a green polo shirt under a navy reefer jacket with gold buttons. His singer's chest gives him a misleading appearance of being stocky so that it is mildly surprising when he first climbs out of his seat in the audience and moves onto the performance area to reveal, with a few large but graceful gestures, a lightness of foot, an ease of movement that betokens the kind of stage performer he once was. One can imagine the master dancing across the stage.

First up is Anna Carmichael, soprano, short and slightly built with her black hair pulled back in a knot. She is eighteen; half-girl, half-woman. As she waits for her accompanist to settle at the piano she smooths her long floral skirt that sits just above a pair of black Doc Marten boots, then girlishly she scratches her knee. I remember Anna from the eisteddfod the Wednesday before, an exquisite little singer of great poise and wit.

Under Maconaghie's expectant gaze she begins now to sing Zerlina's aria from *Don Giovanni*.

Batti, batti, o bel Masetto,
La tua povera zerlina;
Staro qui come agnellina
Le tue botte ad aspettar.
(Beat me, beat me, my Masetto.
Beat your poor Zerlina.
I'll stay here like a lamb
And await your every blow.)

Suddenly, when she sings, this girl seems so much older, so much more worldly and sophisticated. A moment before she was shy and uncertain, now she is coquettish and mocking. Now she has authority. There's that secret self again, the one that pours forth, loudly, boldly, the one that knows things that you don't know, or don't think you know, or didn't know you knew until just then when you opened your mouth and heard yourself ('my voice is so strong, sometimes it frightens me').

Maconaghie listens for one verse and then pulls her up. 'Batti, Batti,' he says. 'The double *t* is almost like a *d*. Let's hear a good Italian *t*.'

She nods. 'Okay.'

A few more lines and he interrupts again. '*Bel Masetto!* Don't drop it between phrases. The Italian *o* – work on that. You'll find that if you get the Italian right you'll sing better.'

'Okay,' she says again, quietly. Her singing voice is loud and thrilling, her speaking voice barely audible, low and deferential.

'And don't rush. Think of the Italian as one long piece of chewing gum, stretching it out. Use your womanly guile, wheedle and sing to your boyfriend.'

'Okay.'

Batti, batti, o bel Masetto
La tua povera Zerlina

Once again he cuts her off. 'Come forward, come forward. Don't be frightened.' He guides her with his arm: 'Come forward, here. We have to make sure people can see us.' And then, turned half to her, half to the audience, he holds the flaps of his jacket open, exposing his chest. 'Here's my heart, here – here it is, don't be afraid. See.' And he opens his arms out wide. It's a charming gesture, from an old pro.

She smiles. 'Okay.'

'And again.'

Batti, batti, o bel Masetto,

La tua povera Zerlina;

Staro qui –

'What are you doing down *here?*' In one fluid movement he has crossed the space and put his hands on her hips and diaphragm. I am still novice enough to register, each time, the familiarity of singing teachers; they adjust the body almost as they would an inanimate musical instrument. Without preamble, inhibition or fuss, they handle the goods. Are the shoulders back? Is the spine straight? Are the knees too stiff and locked? Is the diaphragm free and not pushed up under the ribs? Are the ribs collapsed down on the diaphragm? And then there's the hand on the crown of the head: 'Feel it here, here, *here.*'

I've imagined how I would feel under these conditions. Invaded, ill at ease? Encircled, embattled, coralled?

'Visualise that your voice is actually here –' he gestures '– a foot or eighteen inches in front of you at mouth level.'

'Okay.'

'And remember, step forward. Don't be afraid.'

'Okay.'

'Good girl. Again.'

'*Ah, lo vedo –*'

'No, no. *Ah, lo vedo.*'

'*Ah, lo vedo –*'

'Plant the words more. Like a bad Shakespearean actor.

Overdo it. We can always pull it back. What is the first virtue in a singer? Courage.' To demonstrate his point he holds his arms out wide, exposes his chest and lifts his chin. 'Here I am, shoot your arrows at me. This is the sound I'm coming to make, warts and all, like it or lump it.'

'Okay.'

'From the beginning.'

'Okay.'

Okay, okay, okay, okay.

She begins once again. *Batti, batti, o bel Masetto …* How many times is it now? She's visibly tiring, waning before our eyes. As if in response to this he steps across, moves behind her, takes hold of her hands and lifts her arms into the pose of "The Pride of Erin". Then he begins to dance her forward, gently . . . one and two and one and two . . . and as they continue to dance he begins to sing along with her in a contained, lilting duet, pausing to say at intervals, 'Don't be frightened', or, 'Take a breath there, take a breath there, very good.' Then he lets go of her, drops his arms, stands back a little. 'Very good,' he says quietly. 'Alright, okay, we'll stop there.'

And I want to say, no, no, go on singing, please. Good as she is, his singing is something else. It has a quality of surrender, as if he has long since let go of whatever it is she still clings to. Of course, he is much older, and has none of her nervousness. But still, there is something else there and one day, if she is blessed, she'll have it too.

'Very good,' he says again. 'Well done.' He puts out his hand to her and they shake hands. And the girl walks off, as if in a daze. As she begins to climb the steep aisle of the auditorium he calls up at her. 'These are just thoughts, Anna, just thoughts. Now go home, and think about being a little more on the front foot. Open up the chest and the heart.' He looks down at his paper, looks up again. 'Next?'

9

Seduced by the subtle couplings of the masterclass, in the weeks that follow I sit in on several of Helen Todd's lessons, each time with an increasing sense of the absurdity of my project. I'm an observer making notes, but they're the wrong kind of notes, designed for the eye not the ear, and a poor substitute. The voice creates sound waves, which penetrate the body in such a way and with such startling and immediate effect that no other sensual experience even approximates it. Moreover the dynamic between teacher and pupil is an elusively aural one; a kind of duet, sung in code.

The only way I could crack the code would be to have a lesson myself, and then my code would only be my code and no one else's. And that's not enough. We all want to know everyone else's secrets, not just our own, if only to discover what it is that binds us together – or keeps us apart.

* * *

I arrive one morning at Helen's studio, just before ten. The student this morning is Wayne McDaniel, thirty-six and formerly a professional basketball player with the NBL, now a journalist and commentator with the ABC. I had spoken to Wayne on the phone the night before and sought his permission to come along. Now I sit in a corner of the studio, near the window, and try to be unobtrusive.

Wayne is already there and loosening up. Tall but not freakishly so, he throws his arms in the air and can almost touch the low ceiling. Accustomed to being watched, he is easy and relaxed with my presence. He is a slender, good-looking man with a kind of lithe elegance, even in old jeans, a loose blue striped shirt and stockinged feet. His black head is shaved. With her blonde hair and gently imperious manner there is something Nordic about Helen and in this small room together she and her pupil make a striking pair.

The lesson begins with some scales. Helen explains that while Wayne is a bass baritone she wants him to work on developing his baritone upper notes, on getting rid of the falsetto he is apt to lapse into, his 'Michael Jackson voice': 'We're having a challenge here, getting out of falsetto voice, because every other contemporary popular music singer uses falsetto constantly, and if you listen to it enough you just start doing it, especially the fellas. If Wayne is going to go beyond singing the pop ballad stuff he needs to know his limits and which of them are self-imposed. So we're just trying to get his upper notes into the baritone range of the male voice, not the Michael Jackson shrill voice. Right?' Whenever, throughout the lesson, Helen refers to Wayne's 'Michael Jackson voice' he gives a soft laugh halfway between sheepish and celebratory, and looks at me with a kind of complicit delight.

The vocal exercises begin . . .

* * *

To describe a singing lesson is difficult, if not impossible. For much of the time it can be a monotonous stop-start cycle of scales and exercises, a series of feints and short deft manoeuvres with the breath, punctuated by peremptory commands. Frequently there is a great deal of discussion about breathing and the ribs and diaphragm. Sometimes it's pedestrian; sometimes poetic – 'visualise the note floating up into a golden dome in your head'. Above all it's intensely physical with a hands-on quality about it. The teacher adjusts the back, corrects the angle of the jaw – 'don't push the voice out, let the voice fall out of your face' – places her hands on the solar plexus, feels for the position of the ribs and the diaphragm, squares the hips, puts her palm on the crown of the student's head – 'think big, volume is mental' – and checks for the position of the feet. 'The bulk of the weight needs to be in the middle of the foot. When you get it right, you'll know. You'll feel safe.' There's a lot of face-pulling – 'give me the subtle sneer' – and strange noises, mostly in the warm-up. There is little that is sweet or elegant or delicate. It's a workout.

After his lesson Wayne and I walk to a crowded coffee shop nearby. There, amid the clatter of cutlery and din of conversation he talks into my tape recorder. I note how relaxed he is in this hectic environment, how easily he puts up an invisible screen to shut out whatever distraction hovers around him. Wayne seems to have a quality of deep concentration, of quiet inward focus, and I wonder if it derives from his experience as an athlete, of having to play, year after year, in front of thousands of screaming fans. Or could it be something else?

Why, I ask, does he want to sing?

'Because I always thought I had a voice and now I want to see if I can get it out.'

But why start lessons so relatively late in life? Was there no early encouragement from his family?

Well, he says, he has several brothers, some of them 'into crime and drugs'. He, the youngest, was the most influenced by his mother and his mother was interested in 'all things to do with the voice'.

What does that mean?

'Just anything to do with the voice. Singing, public speaking, broadcasting. And she used to write her own songs. See, I really believe that in my life I'm meant to fulfil the areas in my mother's life that she wasn't able to fulfil. And that gives me meaning for singing.' From time to time, he says, he makes tapes of his latest vocal work and sends them home to his mother in Oakland. He also sends them to his children who live in Adelaide, tapes of spirituals that they can listen to at night in bed.

I tell him that I have recently interviewed an opera singer of note who told me that in his view being a serious singer was in many ways comparable to being a serious athlete. You needed a similar mind-set in order to perform well.

He nods. 'In some ways, being a singer *is* like being an athlete, both are external expressions of who you are. Both are a way to say, here I am, this is me, I've arrived. But there are differences.'

What differences?

Well, he says, basketball is a team game and it's a great

relief at last to be a solo performer. 'I was always very aloof and very … not self-centred, although coaches always say that, just aloof. And I was independent and I didn't always want to be with the team all the time.

'My first coach didn't like that so he worked out on me. He damaged my self-esteem, I had to rebuild it. The other guys looked up to him. See, I looked up to him, but I didn't idolise him. I respected him, but he was just another person, he was just another coach. I often think I would have been better off as a boxer or someone in an individual sport, because that's where my focus was. As an individual.'

'Like in singing?'

'Exactly.'

I tell Wayne that one of the things that interests me about men singing is that it seems a way for them to express their softer side and he responds to this enthusiastically. 'That's right. See, the singing energy for me, looked at in relation to, like athletic energy, the singing energy is more complete, it's more of a merger between masculine and feminine, whereas when I was playing it was so masculine that by the time I was able to nurture those feminine parts of my game I was too old. I was getting to that stage where I was thirty-three, thirty-four and I was developing more subtleties in my game but by that time I only had a couple of years left in me. So, like, singing is the next progression, it's the follow-on from that.

'Now there's, like, two stages I see as being my next areas of growth. One is I have to get the theoretical side down, which is just repetition for me. And the next is getting comfortable with me as a performer, with expressing not just my voice but everything about me – my manners, my idiosyncrasies, movement, body, being comfortable with all that. Rather like being on the basketball court, understand, when I could go on to the court and think, when I was at the top of my game, *I own the game.* That's how I looked at the game, as though the game were mine, that's how I looked at the court. And that's how I need to look at singing.'

10

'I own the game.' Here I am, look at me, acknowledge me, and not just because I'm here, in the spotlight, but because I'm good.

Wayne has a quality that I've observed in many performers, a quality I think of as *sacre egoisme*; literally, a sacred egoism. It's a certain kind of inward concentration on self, and it sounds intensely selfish, but in the sense in which I use it here it refers to something other than blind self-regard. Think of it more as a poetic strategy for survival.

The term *sacre egoisme* was first deployed as part of the language of international diplomacy to describe the belief of men that the welfare of some larger whole justified whatever selfish and duplicitous means were necessary to achieve it. Writ small in the daily life of the individual it becomes a radical form of will bent on self-expression, at whatever cost. Is it always latent, I wonder, or do we acquire it? In suggesting singing lessons to her daughter, did Caroline's mother effect the means of releasing or tapping into something that was already there, or of providing something that before was lacking?

Wherever it comes from, in those who have it the presence of *sacre egoisme* is almost palpable; they seem to exude it from some hidden reserve in their chest, in a way that can both attract and repel. One can observe traces of it in all kinds of performers but I'm beginning to think that it has some special relationship to the voice, to the mysterious potency of song where it becomes transformed, in an almost alchemical way, into something less egoistic and more sacred.

I get a sense of this when eventually I hear Wayne McDaniel sing in public for the first time. We are at an intimate cabaret space known as the Backspace where some of Helen Todd's students are giving a recital. Immediately Wayne begins to sing it is apparent that he is a very good singer indeed. In the middle of the performance space he stands, quite still, barely moving throughout the two spirituals he is there to sing. There is no 'projection' or self-conscious charisma, no flashing white smiles, no playing to the crowd, no swagger, no charm; it is cool, detached and everything is subordinate to the music, to the song. In the intensity of Wayne's focus I sense the egoism which confidently announced itself in his interview ('I *own* that game') but already in his singing another quality has begun to come into play, a kind of ineffable grace that draws the spectator into its magic circle so that what is nominally self-centred becomes spellbindingly inclusive. He cannot of course *own* the song. What he can do is place his whole self at the centre of it and, for a time, merge with it. *Sacre egoisme* gets you to the point where you can get up on your feet in front of a large crowd and make them pay attention. Beyond that, something else, something infinitely more subtle, takes over. But what is it, and why is it so affecting?

11

What happens, I ask Helen, when ordinary, nonprofessional singers sing in public?

'I think they open up a part of themselves that they've pretty well kept closed off for many, many years. Somehow, through singing, they are rediscovering those parts of themselves that gave them great joy when they were a child, and letting them go again, but letting them go in the company of others. In order to let it go at all they have to go very calmly and very deeply inside themselves and that takes a lot of time. And I suspect the nerves are something to do with: *Will it come out?* I mean, that's the normal question for a singer. Is it going to come out? Is it going to come out in the way I would like it to come out?

'And the nerves are also there because you get tempted to interfere all the time. There's this sense of trusting yourself and keeping out of your own way. No matter how good you become, you can still get in your own way.

'And then there's the question of not only will it come out, but how much of it do I want to let out – though in a way they're the same question. I suspect what all my students are going through is finding their own personal depths and how much of this they are prepared to let out. How damaged might they be if they do? It's a very deep well that you have to get down to. It takes a lot of time to get there, a lot of practice. It's like you throw away that sheer nonsense of being a kid, that undisciplined sunny side. We're actually taking ourselves very seriously when we get up in front of an audience, apart from deciding that we're going to open up a piece of ourselves or, as in Wayne's case, a lot of ourselves. Some young singers get a bit of a shock when they realise how bare they've made themselves. Then there's the singer who just gets up and says: "I'm bare, look at me!"

Is she nervous for her students when they perform?

'No'

They're on their own at that point?

'Yes, definitely. They're on their own.'

12

For some reason this reminds me of a story that Beatrice told me.

We are driving home one night and I ask her about the singing group, what it was like before I joined it, and she tells me the story of Julie and how she had haemorrhaged in the middle of a song. They had been standing in the customary circle after a particularly long and intense warm-up. 'Everyone was in tune that night, right from the beginning. It's like everyone came in and, bang, they were straight into it. The warm-up, the sound column, was particularly intense. Things were going really well and for once it all seemed effortless. Then at some point Julie gave a kind of gasp, and I was standing right opposite her and I looked across and there was this red puddle of blood on the floor between her legs. And I'm watching it, sort of mesmerised, and there's this sudden gush and a stream of it runs from between her legs into the puddle, which is just sitting there. And then there's another gush, then another, and two big black clots drop onto the floor. And as I'm looking at her she calmly pulls her T-shirt up over her head – it was a black one – and stuffs it between her legs. And a couple of people crowd around, trying to avoid the clots on the floor. They get her a chair and she sits down and as she sits the T-shirt slips and falls on the floor and the blood begins to seep through the seat of the chair – it was one of those woven rattan seats — and the blood is just seeping through the weave — it was awful — and I look at Julie and she's looking back at me with terror in her eyes. I'll never forget it.'

She pauses at a red light. At this time of night the streets are all but empty. 'Have you ever haemorrhaged?' she asks. As it happens, I have, and I remember that terror, the black sense of being swept away on a tidal swoon of powerlessness, some kind of fecund dying. But I don't want to talk about it now.

'What did you do?' I ask.

'Maria and Kerry drove her to hospital with the T-shirt stuffed between her legs and a spare one from someone else. After she'd gone we looked in the cupboards for cleaning gear and couldn't find a thing. Sarah came back from the old loo with the dirty old towel they hang there and started to mop up the blood. But it had seeped into the cracks and splinters in the old floorboards and wouldn't come out without a scrubbing brush. There were still some brown streaks in the floorboards the next week.'

'What about Julie?'

'She came back eventually.'

'Miscarriage?'

'Yes. And for four months after she couldn't sing a note. But finally she got back into the circle and it was alright.'

I ask a perhaps trivial question, although it's the kind of detail I always want to know. 'Can you remember what you were singing at the time?'

'A George Gershwin medley.'

13

The professional

There's a phrase from Helen Todd's cool assessment that keeps coming back to me, the one about 'keeping out of your own way'. What does this mean? That you are the conduit for the voice but at the same time you are its obstacle? It's a paradox that David Brennan, a resident baritone with Opera Australia elaborates on when I visit him in Sydney later in the month. David is a handsome man in his forties, an eloquent and at times passionate talker and an acute critic of his own art. I want particularly to ask him this: What is it like for the professional? Does it ever get any easier?

'I still have coaching. Most singers do.'

And what is this thing about getting in your own way?

'Ah,' he says, 'this is the nub of it. Because singing is a great paradox. On the one hand it's very technical, you spend years working on your control and most performers are control freaks, they have to be. On the other hand there's a point where you have to just let go of all that and surrender to the music. The performer has to search for the essential truth of the moment, which is, you know, often terribly subtle. And you have to express this without being either over-controlled or self-indulgently "carried away". You have to achieve a kind of detachment, and that's the hard part. The same detachment which is involved in reading a shooting script.

You know: you move over here now, you make sure you're ready to hear a knock on the door now, you don't move too far or you'll be out of the light. You're watching the beat very carefully here because you got out last time. And when you run out of other inspirations, the dependence on technique, on what you've repeated, what you've done technically to get you through that kind of dry moment, that will often be the most triumphant, most successful moment. Because you say: I'm exhausted, my throat's dry, my throat's sore, I don't know if I've got another of those notes in my throat, I was distracted for the last ten minutes and this is the bit where Butterfly hears that Pinkerton isn't coming back again. I can't rewind the reel, so I've just got to go on, I remember what I've got to do, I know what I've got to do . . . and often those kinds of emotionally desiccated moments are the moments that are richest.

'Why? Because you're allowing the music, your body, to speak, without a kind of interpretation, without a . . . I'm groping for the exact word . . . *without being your own intermediary.*'

'You make it sound like there are two of you on stage.'

'Not exactly. But there are two voices that are always there in your head. One of the voices is saying *this is beautiful music and I'd really love to do this and I think I can*, and the other voice is saying *that note wasn't quite right and are you sure you're not leaning over too much, and what's that person saying, and was that a sigh I heard,* and while you're thinking about what you're saying you weren't concentrating on what the music was saying a second ago. And the effect of this is? That you're not in the present moment. *You are not in the present moment.* And being in the present moment is what music is. There is no other purpose to music. It is completely evanescent. It's the ultimate Zen experience. It has no purpose other than to be in the moment, and disappear.'

There's another question I want to ask David Brennan, especially since he's a baritone. What's all this fuss about The Three Tenors? Why the mass response?

'Ah, well,' he says, tilting his head back and sighing with a mixture of exasperation and scorn.' Partly it's an exercise in clever commercial marketing, an essay in the gullibility of the crowd. Some of it is the visceral excitement of responding to a singer at the peak of his powers but the rest of it is a whole lot of bullshit dross, like the three of them singing *'Nessun Dorma'* together.' He groans. 'Wake me up when it's over. I abhor it.'

Is that all? Surely, I remonstrate, there's more. Can tenors be said to have some mystique that baritones lack?

'The tenor voice is the voice of youth,' he replies, after some deliberation. 'Rock singers contrive, no matter what their age, to sound like adolescents. A tenor, even a tenor in his sixties like Pavarotti, sounds like a young man in his prime, a prodigiously talented young man at the peak of his strength.'

'Yes,' I reply, 'but a certain kind of young man. A man who expresses that strength with an enormous amount of refinement, who opens up his heart and gives lyrical voice to the most tender of sentiments.'

'Yes, certainly.'

'Well, it seems to me significant that this spectacle was first launched at a very machismo sporting occasion, the World Cup in soccer. Isn't there something going on here that is not altogether about singing but about, say, the social construction of masculinity? Isn't the sight of Jose Carreras, the most lyrical of tenors singing at a kickfest of headbutters at the very least a striking contrast in masculine styles?' I tell him about Wayne McDaniel and his allusion to his "feminine" side.'

'Well, this is an interesting question, a very interesting question. I mean I do meditate on what it is to be a male at this time in history, in the light of a society which has been heavily influenced by feminism. I watch my son, who is now twenty, growing up, and attempting to find his own masculinity, and I don't know what to say to him. I am incredibly lucky. I have my own voice I am allowed to sing with and exercise my own voice, my own unchallengeable masculine voice, and this is a way of finding, or at least acting – playing – my masculinity. I read somewhere that there's a Japanese verb, *to play*, which is, in the mouths of the samurai, to do. Instead of *doing* something, you *play* something.'

'You play the part?'

'No, no. The verb *play* is used in the sense of *to do*. It's an extremely interesting thing because what I do is play *and* do, and I can be the impermissible male, in a sense. And so can they.'

'They?'

'So can those Three Tenors. But equally, I would ask: what is happening when we listen to a powerful soprano voice? Isn't there a similarly androgynous appeal at play? Perhaps even more so with the mezzo-soprano who sings trouser roles – Octavian in *Der Rosenkavalier* and so on. There are an extraordinary number of those. A good half of the mezzo-soprano roles are written for women who have to impersonate men. But let's carry this further. Let's look at an operatic soprano, or an operatic female singer. Doesn't *she* take on much of the masculine? The strength, the capacity to fill the hall with her voice, the capacity to take charge of her own destiny and express it? Isn't she every bit as androgynous as the tenor?'

'Yes,' I say, 'but, traditionally women are expected to sing, as part of their ornamental and recreational function – the courtesan, the geisha, and so on. It's not such a break from traditional roles to listen to a woman lament her fate as it is to hear a burly male pouring his heart out in the upper register.'

'I don't know about that. Which traditions are we speaking of? In many cultures it was the role, indeed the privilege of the men *only* to express the moral and political leadership of their society or tribe by singing on all ritual occasions.'

This, I have to concede, is true.

Part 2

1

Machiavelli's river

Not long after the Port Arthur shootings in 1996, when a mood of intense gloom hung over the city of Hobart, I stood in the historic Salamanca Market area by the waterfront and listened to the Sisongke Choir sing a number of slow and affecting African laments. It was a sunny Saturday morning and the market was congested with people and a display of colourful stalls. Dressed informally in black T-shirts, forty or so members of the choir stood on the grass verge and sang hauntingly in African dialects that none of us at that time understood, although this did not make it any the less affecting.

thina sizwe
thina sizwe sintsundu
sikelela
sikelela izwe lethu

Thina sizwe is a song about dispossession; a demand that what has been taken away from us be restored. After only a few minutes I found it unbearable and moved away but the voices of the choir carried on the sea breeze and seemed to waft behind me.

The second time I hear Sisongke sing is in the ornate Town Hall, a minor Georgian masterpiece of pastel blue and gold with Grecian urns on pedestals set in arched wall recesses, a parquet floor, scarlet seats, a huge gilt mirror in baroque gold leaf and crystal chandeliers. On either side of the stage, above the bronze pipes of the organ and painted on the wall in gold are two of the Muses, one with her books, the other with her artist's palette. Neither is carrying a lyre.

The Sisongke Choir is here for a special concert with visiting singer Valanga Khoza. A former member of SASO, Steve Biko's South African Student Organisation, Valanga fled from South Africa at the age of sixteen and moved to Swaziland as a political refugee. He completed his formal education in the US and now lives in Melbourne where he makes his living travelling Australia as a performer and running choral workshops for schools and community groups. This is not the first time Valanga has worked with Sisongke and he is a great favourite with his long dreadlocks pulled back in a bunch, his tiny Zulu 'piano' the *kalimba* that he holds in one hand and uses to tune the choir, and a great line in sardonic charm. In the finale he joins the choir in a stirring performance of *Nkosi Sikelele* ('God Bless Africa'), until recently the anthem of 'terrorists', now the official anthem of the new Republic of South Africa. The wall behind Valanga is dominated by three lifesize portraits from the nineteenth century, chief among them Robert 4th Earl of Buckinghamshire and Lord Hobart, Secretary of State for the Colonies. The colonial tide is still turning.

But why so much African music? Since Africans are not a large ethnic group in Hobart, each time I heard Sisongke sing I became more curious. Why African? How did this come about?

2

In 1994 black activist Siphiwo Lubambo was living in exile
in Sydney. A former choirmaster in South Africa and now
cultural ambassador at large for the African National Con-
gress, Siphiwo was invited to Hobart for three weeks in
February to give a series of singing workshops for the public.
This was an initiative of John McQueenie, thenArts officer
for the Tasmanian Trades and Labor Council.

John McQueenie gives me a vivid account of Siphiwo's
first workshop, a one-off at Risdon Prison. For some weeks
Siphiwo had run a programme at Brisbane's Boggo Road
Gaol but time at Risdon was limited. For an hour and a
half he attempted to persuade a group of Risdon inmates
to sing but they were unmoved, refusing to utter a note. As
he spoke they began to make jokes and nudge one another.
Singing was for poofs, they said. Well, said Siphiwo, in
his culture singing was a mark of manhood and men were
proud of their singing prowess. No response. Siphiwo kept
talking. He told them about the work of the ANC in Africa
and how he had been a weapons instructor there. At that
point the mutinous undertow of murmuring began to sub-
side. He was asked: had he ever killed a man? Sensing that
his credibility had suddenly been enhanced and sensing also
a change in the mood of the gathering, Siphiwo declined to
answer the question. Instead he began to turn the discussion
around and back to the subject of singing. With only ten

minutes of the session left he at last managed to persuade the men to make a few sounds, to try a few vocal exercises in a simple warm-up. But by the time they were ready to sing, time had run out.

Siphiwo had better luck in his principal forum for the summer, a series of workshops for the labour movement. It was John McQueenie's hope that these would result in the formation of a community choir and with this in mind the workshops were offered intensively over the summer break with over one hundred and forty people turning up for three to six sessions a week. Much of the instant success of the project can be attributed to Siphiwo's flamboyant and ener-gising style and what seems to have been an almost immedi-ate political rapport with the majority of the attendees. Says Victoria Rigney, now performance manager of Sisongke: 'We were always profoundly aware of the situation in South Africa at that time. Siphiwo taught us several songs in three South African languages and every now and then he would stop and tell us a story about his days as an activist.' Unsur-prisingly, some connected to the politics of the scene more than others. 'I was deeply affected by Siphiwo's stories,' said one choir member, 'but yet there were always some people in the room who weren't listening. You know, they'd be hum-ming a little tune . . . "

At the end of the three weeks Siphiwo had pulled the group together for a sell-out concert at Hobart's elegant old Theatre Royal. This proved to be an occasion of some intensity. It was the year leading up to the elections in South Africa, public interest was high and the choir performed

Nkosi Sikelele, still an underground anthem. At the end of the concert the singers and audience were linked by telephone to the ANC office in Soweto and John McQueenie spoke on stage to representatives there. I heard many accounts of that evening, summed up by Victoria as 'incredible. It was very moving.'

When Siphiwo returned to Sydney the local singers voted to continue in some form. They decided they wanted to become a choir and named it Sisongke, a Xhosa word meaning 'side by side'. Victoria: 'None of us knew anything about music, or choral direction. We just knew that we wanted to keep doing what we'd been doing.' A few of the group took on the work of organising a choir and finding a musical director. They approached Micheál McCarthy at the Tasmanian Conservatorium of Music, an Irishman with a wealth of choral experience which included training in Hungary in the Kodaly method. McCarthy agreed to take them on. The next step was to find a venue and eventually they settled on the Quaker Meeting House at the Friends School which seemed more than appropriate. Officially the choir came into being in June 1994 with joint sponsorship from Community Aid Abroad and the TTLC which had applied for and been given Australia Council funding for community cultural development.

To say that there were teething problems is an understatement. From the beginning many in the choir were at odds with the TTLC. 'Things,' to quote Victoria Rigney, 'were a bit scratchy' and the differences came to a head the following February. Victoria again: 'It was one of those summer concerts in the park, a scorching hot day. One of the choir members introduced a song we had learned about East Timor and she said the Australian government was exacerbating the position there at present. Then I introduced a song called "Keep on Walking Forward" and dedicated it to Bob Brown who had just been arrested in the Tarkine Valley and was in gaol that weekend. The audience cheered, and so did the choir, but that was the beginning of the end with the TTLC. We had the most immense fallout the following week. People in the audience had gone straight to the TTLC and accused us of being anti-government, pro-Green, environmental terrorists, you name it.

'Perhaps, looking back, we were a bit naive. There was a strong rift in Tasmania between the Greens and the Labor Party and we had somehow played right into it. We learned the hard way. We wanted our songs to be political but with a small *p*, and not to be aligned with any party. We also agreed then that we wanted our songs to speak for themselves, and that we should avoid provocative introductions.'

At this point the choir embarked on a new phase. Its members were no longer under the auspices of the TTLC and Community Aid Abroad; they were independent and on their own and they had to decide on some kind of rationale. Why were they singing? What did they want to achieve? What should their repertoire be? Were they serious musicians or were they a glee club? Victoria: 'There was this ongoing debate between those who want to have fun and those who want to progress musically, and how do you just keep it in the middle there somehow. In the early days we got frustrated. Micheál would stop a lovely song and just want to go over and over and over again and again and even his most dedicated followers would think, 'Oh, come on! Just let us sing, we just want to sing it!' He had to modify that a bit, and he did. We also came to see that the Siphiwo concert had largely succeeded because of its emotional appeal and now we had to improve musically if we were to continue. Once when Valanga came to do a workshop with us Micheál was sitting in the back row, writing. Someone asked why he wasn't joining in and I told them to go and watch what he was doing. He was writing out the songs in four parts, as Valanga sang them, so we could keep them in the repertoire after the workshop. A lot of people in the choir can't read music and to work with someone with those skills is a real experience. So those people who at first resisted the different leadership style came to see how fortunate we were to have this talent in our midst.'

Micheál McCarthy: 'If Sisongke just went to sing for fun all the time they wouldn't still be interested in it after two years. Fun is important, but fun is serious work. A sense of play has to be part of the rehearsal process but it is not for fun's sake, it is for the sake of the music. I prefer it if the sense of fun comes from the achievement. The paradox is that to maintain the sense of fun you have to continue to develop. If you aim *only* to have fun you may well lose interest. Part of my role is to be aware of this. There can be a certain tension if members of the choir want only to give performances. How can they give performances unless they work hard?'

One of the most fraught of the early issues was repertoire. As Micheál McCarthy says, 'Community choirs are made up of people with particular expectations.' He makes the point that many professional musicians will 'play whatever is put in front of them when it is their job to do that. Amateurs are different.' Victoria: 'We would bring along songs we loved, perhaps ballads with a human rights bent, and Micheál could see that they wouldn't work musically for the big choir. He would bring along music suitable for a choir but it mightn't be what we wanted from the political or emotional angles. I remember Micheál brought along a song, beautifully arranged. It wasn't quite a hymn but was a kind of "spring has come" celebration and it mentioned God at least once, maybe twice, and there were people there who just said, "No, we won't sing that, we are not going to sing about God." And that was the only time I thought he was going to walk out the door and leave us. Instead, with a look of complete exasperation on his face he walked to the back of the rehearsal room and stood there for a moment. Then he turned around and came back and said, "Just explain why it is that you will sing about God in Zulu, in Xhosa. You do know, don't you, what *Nkosi Sikelele* means?" And people thought that *Nkosi Sikeleli* was beyond critique . . . and rightly so. It's our favourite song and we do our best and all of that, but it *is* about God. And a lot of people said, "Oh, okay, fine."

'So there was a bit of a gap there about where he was coming from and where we were coming from. It was all part of our evolution. After that we came up with a repertoire committee where we'd work things out. And that was how we all had to grow together. And some of the more radical people who didn't want that degree of formality or process left. But in fact the repertoire committee has now lapsed, we don't need it any more because now we tend to have a lot more mutual trust and understanding.

'It's all that connectedness stuff. First you work it out in the choir among yourselves and then you kind of branch out into the broader community. We decided to look at what music there is in Hobart and began to develop The Hidden Music of Hobart project. We've just done our first one which is a Latvian song, *Put Vejinz*. Members of the Latvian community came and taught it to us and they perform it with us now, on stage in national dress. The project relates to our human rights emphasis and we have a statement of unity about it that says that this is what we are all about. But we are also about recognising cultural and musical diversity within Hobart, and even within the choir we will continue to search out pieces and learn about the communities from which they come. It's a wonderful idea but a hell of a lot of work. To start with it created a lot of stress; people began to feel it was becoming too much like work and not enough like fun. We had to have a meeting and sort out our priorities. But somehow it always works out. That's the interesting thing about the choir as an entity, the way in which the whole is greater than its parts. It's a bit like Machiavelli's river; you can put obstacles in its course but it seems to find its way around them.'

1. *The Choral Singer (i)*

MARNIE ROGERS, *member of Sisongke Choir, Hobart.* 'Why do I want to sing? What a question! The real question is: why *don't* other people sing?

'Okay, okay, why do I sing? Well . . . there's a part of me that feels a bit guilty for not being more out there and in the world. I've always been in the world and I was brought up to think I had to participate in the world. And because I don't have a job or any children around any more, and all that sort of stuff, I feel I'm not in the world. I used to be politically active and now I'm not. I really don't care who's in politics anymore – sort of vaguely, but only a bit. And the choir works on both the personal and the political level. I get all these lovely endorphin hits for myself and at the same time, because we're singing the kind of songs we're singing, about human rights, that's my political action.

'But even if it weren't these political songs I could still justify it by saying I contribute to the harmony of the planet. How? Well, I just assume that anything that has a harmonious factor to it rather than a dishar-monious one is adding a little to the total harmony of the whole. And I couldn't do it on my own, I couldn't sing on my own; I seem to need to butt up against something. I like to know that I have a role in some-thing bigger than I am. I need to feel part of a whole.

'And we sing everything in four parts and that's a great satisfaction, singing in harmony. I need to see – the world needs to see – something in union, instead of scattered and disparate. And I think that's what happens when you have parts. You have four people supposedly singing something different but they're making a whole at the same time. I also want a few male voices as well as female voices; I don't like all male or all female choirs. They're not whole.

'There's a fascinating group exercise I should tell you about that relates to this thing called harmony. It's an exercise that people who run workshops sometimes do called "the vocal wheel". Eight people lie head to head in a group, in a circle, like the spokes of a wheel. In a big room you might have six groups or more. You lie on the floor or stand around – it might take an hour – and you just make any sound you feel like, nonsense noises, shrieks and groans – people carry on and carry on. And it all starts by coming out of the bottom of your stomach, real gut stuff, all the anger and vomit and you get into doing primal stuff, it might be crying or gurgling or whatever, baby stuff, and then you come through that, as if you were working through the chakras as sound. And then, after a while, people start listening to each other. Whoever is running the workshop might say: Now, listen to the person next to you, pick up on that. That goes on for a while, then you start listening across the room and after about, say, forty-five minutes or so, people have come out of that and they're actually into some exquisite symphonic sound. It sounds like a composed symphony and everyone has a part in it, like they're an instrument. No words, just sound. In the end it all just comes into an extraordinary harmony. It works every time.

'And the interesting question is, will cacophony always end up in harmony if you let it go long enough? I don't know, I've only had three experiences, but I suspect that if you set up an occasion for people to sing they will eventually attune themselves to one another, if you give them long enough.'

2. Choral Fixation

I like the Sisongke story. I like what it says about the politics of culture in general and of art in particular. Getting together to sing is not a straightforward matter; all kinds of value-laden issues come into play. It makes me curious about the histories of other large choirs, like the Sydney Gay and Lesbian Choir, and curious about the very institution itself. What is the originary moment of the massed community choir? How did it get to be one of the most resilient of our cultural forms, one that can always be relied upon to reflect the character of its time? Among the many accounts I am drawn to one proffered by music historian Henry Raynor in his book, *Music and Society Since 1815* (1976). Raynor tells the story of the Berlin court musician Carl Friedrich Fasch who in 1787 suddenly realised that his salary had been seriously devalued by the Seven Year War. Seeking to

augment it by a few extra-curricular activities Fasch begins
by conducting a singing class for wealthy bourgeois wives,
one of whom, the wife of an official in the Prussian War
Ministry, offers her garden for rehearsals. Thus is born the
Berlin *Singakademie*. Four years later it accepts men into its
membership (I would like to have heard the debate on this)
and soon after gives its first public performance.

Over the next forty years similar choirs spring up
throughout Germany and Switzerland and later in France,
Austria and England, more often than not with agendas
that are other than musical. In Switzerland, Hans Georg
Nageli, a disciple of the educationalist and social reformer
Pestalozzi, believes that singing in groups will produce a
sense of social unity and purpose. In 1805 he forms the
Zurich *Singinstitut* and from this and his subsequent work
there develop a number of festivals, not only in large cities
but in small towns and even in villages. Nageli's work, like
the whole of the Pestalozzi movement, coincides with and
is said to express the spirit of the new political organisations
of Switzerland which give the nation its modern structure
as a democratic state.

Throughout Europe both the choirs and the prolifer-
ating festivals become self-propagating. A combination
of local patriotism and the competitive spirit allied to an
appetite for the new ensures their spread. Many compos-
ers, including Mendelssohn, become enthusiastic support-
ers of their activities. 'The appeal of choral music in Ger-
man-speaking Europe,' writes Raynor, 'is that it allows each
individual member, man or woman, to become involved in

the thoroughly democratic processes that are denied to him or her in political life.' In the choral societies all decisions, democratically arrived at, are the results of general votes of all the members and this gives the choral societies political implications unwelcome to the authorities. The fact that large and efficient organisations can function successfully by democratic methods suggests a criticism of the authoritarianism by which central European states are controlled. Such choral organisations provide a valuable lesson in practical democracy; as such they become hemmed in by police regulations. They are of course almost entirely middle class, apart from activities like the work of the German musician Joseph Mainzer who institutes large-scale singing classes for the poor in Paris.

This might sound like a simple-minded Whig view of history in which music and democracy march arm in arm along the golden path of Progress, but Raynor is alert to the murkier outcomes of the industrial revolution. To begin with it wreaks havoc on rural families with devastating effects on traditional folk singing. People who had once worked at home where they sang freely now move to factories in the towns where the deafening noise of the new machines drowns them out. A musicologist's survey of factory workers in Lancashire in the 1850s shows that parents are passing on a rapidly dwindling repertoire of songs to their children.

At this historical moment John Wesley and the Methodist Revival bring group singing into the realm of the common worker. Wesley wants hymns which the simplest and most illiterate people can remember and sing. As in Lutheranism the whole congregation is to sing and not, as in the Church of England at that time, sit silently while others sing to it. Wesley knew that when individual men and women sing together they become a community, a congregation. Methodism converts widely in the new industrial towns among a depressed and degraded working-class. And it is at least arguable, writes Raynor, that 'music attracted people to Methodism as much as Methodism attracted people to music'.

Many factory owners encourage the development of work-site choirs, seeing in these an encouragement to a sober and pious (and with luck, docile) workforce. Some of the more enlightened (or more shrewd) pay for a weekly singing class in work time and contribute to expenses: sheet music, travel to eisteddfods and so on. Dickens' father-in-law and music critic for the *Daily News*, George Hogarth writes of the proliferation of choral societies among workers: 'their wages are not squandered in intemperance, and they become happier as well as better'. Thus begins a tradition that sees every Lancashire factory, every Welsh colliery have its own choir (and band) and community singing practices become entrenched in ways that live on in the massed singing of the terraces at English football games.

Factors other than religion, however, begin to play a part in the growth of community choirs. During the last half of the nineteenth century the increasing prosperity of the middle class combined with technological changes means that middle-class women have less work to do at home, yet wives and daughters are not allowed by the conventions of the times to work outside the home or to participate in public and political activities. They take to joining choral groups until, with the beginning of the women's emancipation movement, and its eventual acceptance, these musical organisations begin to decline. Today, however, in the 1990s, they are in revival. Why?

3. The Pied Piper

In February 1995 Julie Clarke wrote an article for *HQ* magazine which looked at the new fad for singing in a cappella groups. Five years ago there were two such groups in Sydney, now there are over sixty, and these are just the ones we know about (and they don't include three or four people who've decided just to get together in their living rooms and sing once a week). Called 'Praise the Lord and Pass the Lipstick', Clarke's article focused on the best known of the Sydney groups, Cafe at the Gate of Salvation, and the work of its founder and musical director Tony Backhouse.

If there is one person who could be said to be emblematic of the singing revival it's Backhouse, truly a man with a mission. Regarded by many as Australia's finest gospel singer, since the early nineties he has run voice workshops all over Australia in the belief that singing is 'fundamental to being human' and everyone should do it. 'Everyone can sing,' he asserts. 'It's only fear and cultural conditioning that stops us. It's the first way we express ourselves as babies. It makes work go better, helps breathing and changes brain chemistry resulting in feelings of joy.' All music has the power to change things, he says, but especially singing: 'You can't sing without being changed.' Backhouse is passionate in his espousal of DIY. 'In our culture singing is left to the experts, singers with a capital S. It hasn't always been like that. In the good old days everyone sang around the piano, chortling over moonbeams and kisses, dreams and wedding bells. These days we're encouraged not to sing in the rain, on the plane, or anywhere that others can complain. That's a pity because singing is a primal form of self-expression. You don't need to sit down at a piano. It's the most fundamental form of musical expression there is. It opens up the heart.'

The singing that Backhouse is pledged to is black gospel singing because, as he says, 'It's not about the voice, it's about the soul, the spirit.' Not surprisingly his views are reflected in the members of the Cafe. When interviewed by Clarke a significant number of them cited spiritual reasons for joining the choir. 'Every so often I feel spiritually starved, as if there is a special kind of food that I need to be fully alive' (Taffira Hall, 31). Another: 'Singing with the choir is a blessing that provides regular experiences of absorption and transcendence' (David Hall, 38). According to Judy Backhouse: 'Some conventional Christians are confused by us. They ask, "What church are you from?"'

The Cafe is not from any church; it represents a kind of New Age eclecticism. Anything goes. Not the least interesting thing about the choir is it's betokening of the emergence of a new sensibility, grounded in Baby Boomers and Generation Xers alike. Clarke tentatively defines it as a kind of postmodern spirituality; it is irreverent, eclectic, hip and tolerant – qualities encapsulated in Backhouse's own manifesto. 'Jesus,' he says, 'is our culture's prevailing metaphor for spiritual excellence, and while the religion built around this metaphor has an unstable and unsound history, Jesus' contribution (non-violent, non-sexist, non-racist, to say the least) is a wonderful thing. I feel comfortable working with the Christian metaphor. Others in the group re-translate the words we sing into political terms or more general spiritual terms. There has to be a place for non-specific spirituality.'

There has to be a place for non-specific spirituality. Each time I read this sentence, I am struck by it. What is 'a non-specific spirituality' and is the singing group one of its natural sites? Here is Stephanie Dowrick, a former student of Tony Backhouse's who accompanied him on a gospel singing tour of the American south.

4. Gospel

Through many dangers, toils and snares,
I have already come:
'Tis grace has brought me safe thus far
And grace will lead me home.

STEPHANIE DOWRICK: *at home: Monday December 9, 1996.* 'If I had a life to choose I would prefer to be a musician than to be a writer. Why? Because words are always limiting, inevitably limiting, aren't they? And because the contact with the audience is just so *immediate*, and because through music you're reaching to people's hearts in a *very* direct way. You transcend the self through the music, and you transcend the limitations between self and other through the music. There is not another art form that does it so powerfully.

'The liberation of group singing for me is that it's an art form where I don't have to be the best, where my ego is not involved, where I don't have to be ever hoping for a solo, or to shine; where all I need do is experience the music- experience the music rather than experience my ego through the music. That's the most amazing liberation.

'Why gospel? Well, several reasons. It's a music of worship. That is really important to me. I like the uninhibited worship of it. I like the fact that it's music that comes out of suffering, and transforms suffering, because it developed from the old Negro spirituals. It's extremely forgiving music – I mean it's forgiving of the people who sing it in as much as you can do all kinds of things with it so that even if you haven't got a great voice you can still sing it – and, in its actual intention, it's forgiving. I find that really attractive.

'I sang it in classes for five or six months before I went on a gospel tour of the US with Tony Backhouse and a group of other gospel singers. When I started I did feel somewhat embarrassed about being in a group of people I didn't know, doing something that I felt very uncertain about, but I'd just had cancer and I thought, hell, you know, I'm just going to sing, because I might die and, I thought, my inhibitions are of no consequence here whatsoever.

'I had sung when I was young and I'd loved singing, really

loved it. And even after school I'd sing sometimes but in the intervening years I hadn't sung and I'd really, really missed it. 'I haven't got a very good voice now, I truly haven't. But for me singing is about surrendering yourself and just accepting what you've got. It exemplifies the parable of the talents which I think is a very important parable, teaching us to make use of what we've got. That we're all given many talents and to say, No thank you, you didn't give me a good enough one here, God, so I won't sing because you didn't give me whoever's voice – well, it would seem like a crazy waste.

'Having cancer was the catalyst. It absolutely propelled me into music. I did a workshop with Frankie Armstrong when I had just come out of hospital and somebody there told me that Tony Backhouse was giving classes. So I started going immediately, with some anxiety and shyness. I didn't talk to people much at the beginning. I'd have my cup of tea in the break by myself but I didn't mind that either. It was just the most enormous relief to be singing. And I was feeling very, very stressed at the time, stressed and distressed. I was parched and the music was like water.

'Tony is a brilliant teacher. He doesn't make you do a lot of exercises and repetition. You *sing*. He teaches everything in four parts, straight off, and you just sing. He doesn't get very technical yet he produces the most stunning effects. He brings people's voices out just wonderfully.

'What do people get from this? I can only speak for myself. I get numbers of things. One is the opportunity to pray through music. It is, for me, a very intense and radiant form of meditation. When I sing I really try to allow

myself to recognise and experience that I'm singing in praise
of God. Then there's also this amazing sense of being connected to other people – who may be complete strangers to
you – only through the music. I really like that. You can feel
a kind of kinship of soul with people who, at the end of the
class, just go off in their different directions. I like making
connections that are not forged through words and discussion. And I feel healed by the music. From the outset I have
felt the music working on me. I felt that most particularly
when we were travelling in the south singing every day. Singing every day, and hearing great gospel music sung by others
made the most enormous difference to me. I think it cured
me of cancer. Spending all those hours in black churches,
praying intensely with people who are utterly uninhibited in
their expression of devotion, it released me somehow. That
experience of singing was so intense, letting the music come
through us, move us, every single day.

'I haven't in my own therapy practice recommended singing to people as therapy. But last year when I was having this
dreadful time I did some somatic (body-oriented) therapy.
There were days when I went to see my therapist and I was
so depressed I could barely speak. And several times – he's
a wonderful singer, this guy – several times he just stood
up and started to sing. And I would force myself up, and I
would also sing. I remember one memorable occasion when
I couldn't speak and we were sitting in this complete kind
of doldrum, and I stood up and started to sing, and then he
started to sing with me and I moved myself out of the pits.

'I think it's partly to do with your breathing; it's also

partly posture; it's partly moving your mind, as you do in meditation, on to something very focused. But singing is more energetic than meditation is. There's so much energy to it, and I think you can tune into a collective energy which reminds you that you are not alone. Of course, when you are depressed, that's when it's hardest to sing. But I had to — it was a *huge* act of will, a huge act of will to do it at all. It felt to me in some moments like a choice between life and death.'

Part 3

1

The Heart's Ear

What is the secret of the human voice and where can we expect to find an answer to that question? Is it purely an organic phenomenon to do with the release of endorphins, or does it connect us to a more spiritual dimension? Who is the oracle here: the physician or the metaphysician?

In *Great Singers on Great Singing* (1982) the former bass baritone with The Metropolitan in New York, Jerome Hines conducts over thirty interviews with opera singers of international standing. Almost all of these are exclusively devoted to issues relating to the soft palate, the uvula, the sinuses, the diaphragm and even the width of the face. Occasionally, someone like Renata Tibaldi will declare enigmatically that 'singing is ninety per cent in the mind' but for the most part one gains the impression that the chief artistic consultant of professional singers is their ear, nose and throat physician.

The most controversial of these who has advised many singers is the distinguished French physician Alfred Tomatis (b 1920). You might think that any survey of the work of Tomatis would begin with a treatise on the larynx, or the tongue, but it is Tomatis's contention that the key to the voice is in the ear. If we cannot hear we cannot speak or sing. Mystics like the Sufi scholar Pir Hazrat Inayat Khan teach that the ear and not the eye is the primary sense organ out of which all other senses develop. Hearing is the first of the senses to be awakened in the womb, at around five months, and the sound of the mother's voice is the first sense imprint on the new self.

Over a period of forty years the research of Albert Tomatis focused on these aural beginnings and attempted to unravel their skein of significance within a medical model. Tomatis – whose father, not coincidentally, was an opera singer – devoted his career to analysing the effect that various components of sound, including singing, have on our bodies. His most radical theory is the concept of cortical charge, that it is the primary function of the ear to provide the cells of the body with electrical stimulation and that the cells of Corti deep in the inner ear transform sound waves into electrical input. The function of the ear is to listen and the function of listening is to charge the brain with electrical potential and hence to charge the nervous system. Sounds, especially the ones we make ourselves as singers and speakers, are a kind of primal energy food. This of course is something that most people know intuitively which is why the first thing a fatigued worker does on arriving home is to listen to music or begin herself to sing around the house. It has been Tomatis's life work to attempt to demonstrate or explicate this intuition in scientific terms.

One of the best known anecdotes about his work as a consultant physician concerns an order of Benedictine monks in a monastery in the south of France which was in a state of decline. A number of physicians had been called in to diagnose the prevailing malaise. One had suggested that the traditional sleep pattern of the monks of from three to four hours a night was insufficient and suggested an increase to six hours or eight. A second consultant recommended adding more animal protein to their diet which was almost wholly vegetarian but for a little fish. The fact that the monks had maintained their prodigious workloads on such a diet since the twelfth century was not considered significant. Fatigue, lethargy, depression and physical ill health continued to increase. After a time Tomatis, who had a villa nearby and who knew the Abbe was called in on an informal basis. After studying the daily routine of monks before and after the modernising reforms of Vatican Two, Tomatis came to a single conclusion. He recommended that the monks return to the practice they had abandoned post Vatican Two of meeting together eight and nine times a day to sing Gregorian chant. Singing together, he said, would create a mental and emotional focus that would bring the monastery group field into harmony and resonance as a community, as well as profoundly recharging the energy of individual monks. Within six months, he claims, there was a dramatic improvement in the life of the monastery.

Would any singing have achieved the same effect? Not according to Tomatis. The singing must be of a particularly powerful kind, of which Gregorian chant is exemplary. It is partly the effect of overtones on the nervous system, partly the elongated vowel sounds of Gregorian and the special breathing practices that enable them. The slowest possible breathing, as required by the elongated vowels of the chant, is a sort of respiratory yoga that leads to a state of tranquillity and balance. Doing this in company with others, and at the same rate, enhances the effect. Symmetry is achieved. Respiratory and heart rates slow down and come into alignment. It is the same sensation, says Tomatis, when you are listening to a great singer. 'You mimic him because, first of all, he excites all of your higher proprioceptor responses, and then you dilate to breathe strongly with him. You become sure of the note that comes next. It is you who sings the note and not him. He invites you to do it in your own skin.' (Tomatis, 1990.) This is the phenomenon of so-called entrainment, where systems come into alignment, as in Huygens' famous pendulum experiment. When individuals sing or chant together, everyone is in a sense tuning together. They lock in, first on the physical plane and then, if you have a mystical cast, on the spiritual plane to achieve a kind of union. Singing in church is a form of spiritual entrainment. Singing the national anthem or any patriotic song is a form of political and social entrainment (something the Nazis and all propagandists understand only too well). The musicologist Jill Purce tells of running a summer school for teachers and discussing the problem of school assemblies. Traditionally the school assembly was a time for singing the school song and/or some kind of hymn. In recent times both practices have become problematical but it is Purce's argument that it doesn't matter what you sing, the important thing is to sing *something* since the real aim of any assembly is to tune pupils and teachers into something larger than themselves so that the activities of the school can be harmonious. This reminded me of the observation by a teacher of my acquaintance that the most harmonious schools with the least discipline problems have, in his experience, been those with the most developed musical culture and, in particular, a great emphasis on mass participation in school choir.

Much of Tomatis's work turns on the distinction between hearing and listening. Listening is the key to everything; it is paying attention, it takes you out of yourself and is the first step in making a connection with others. The desire to listen is the human's most ontological desire, says Tomatis, since it is the basis of his desire to communicate. The foetus's first communication is with the world outside, with the sound of his mother's voice. In the womb 'listening to the mother's voice remains the most fundamental perception'. The autistic child, for example, is able to hear but unable to listen. Stuttering is a listening disorder; dyslexia is a listening disorder. The anxious or neurotic subject is blocked in his or her listening. Hearing refers only to the physical capabilities of the ear; listening, including self-listening, is the first step in understanding the self and communication with others. In the broadest sense and on the highest level it is the auditory function of the psyche. And learning to sing is pre-eminently learning to listen, to hear the notes in your own voice, to hear them in others and then to bring them into the relationship – for example, harmony – that you desire.

In all of this the role of high frequencies is crucial. The thing first heard by the foetus is the voice of the mother, a faint and slightly strident solo in the symphony of bodily sounds. It is a sound which comes to us filtered naturally by bone conduction in some of the high frequencies. These are replicated in certain music, and instruments like bag-pipes and trumpets which is why these instruments are used to excite and energise in, say, military charges. It is the bones that sing. The voice essentially excites bone conduction, giving the impression that sound originates from outside or beyond the body. Here is a purely organic explanation for the sensation one sometimes has, when singing, of the ethereal, of being taken out of oneself.

I find myself greatly intrigued by the character of Tomatis who was a driven man with something of a messianic sense of mission. In this he is at times reminiscent of that mad genius Wilhelm Reich, although unlike Reich he has been greatly honoured in his own scientific community despite being controversial. He regarded himself as no mere technician and was a devout Catholic, making a considerable leap beyond the purely technical aspects of his work to the realms of the metaphysical. 'When you are singing, it is God singing with your body like an instrument,' he writes. 'It is the universe that speaks, and we are the machines to translate the universe,' and so on. The leap he makes is a purely personal one since he in no way demonstrates it. It is true, nevertheless, that in all ages and in all cultures there has been a profound connection between singing and religious or ritual practice. And, as leading disciples of Tomatis such as the US music therapist Don Campbell are quick to emphasise, the various forms of sacred chant that occur across a range of cultures occur in high frequencies. In Tomatis's terms they are a form of high-frequency audition therapy indispensable to the health of the priestly and sha-manic caste, and an essential part of their spiritual medi-cine. We see it in the Indian yoga of sound, mantra yoga, in Tibetan horns and cymbals, Zen gongs, Christian church organs and steeple bells, Hindhu bhajan singing and in the extraordinary Tibetan practices of overtone chanting.

2

Music in the ancient world was a mysterious and powerful tool for the attunement of body and psyche. 'The wise,' writes Inayat Khan, 'considered the science of sound to be the most important science in every condition of life.' It is, as Joachim Ernst Berendt reminds us, 'the Word made Flesh of the Bible; the *nada* or soundless sound of the *Upanishads*; the *nam* or *Gurbani* of the Sikh Adi Granth; the *kalma-i-ilahi* or inner sound of the Koran; and the *saute surmadi* or *hu* of Sufism. It is also synonymous with Plato's Logos, with the Pythagorean music of the spheres. Buddhism knows it as *Fohat* while Chinese mysticism recognises it as the Kwan-Yin-Tien or the Melodious Heaven of Sound.' (*The Third Ear*, 1988)

In every culture ritual singing and chanting is employed as a means of awakening a higher consciousness. In Hinduism, for example, the greatest of the arts is singing, the shortest route to the spiritual heights because it is the most direct expression of a person's spirit. Nor is this belief confined purely to Eastern mysticism. Martin Luther believed so strongly in the power of singing to arouse the 'sad, sluggish and dull spirit' that he made it the basis of his reformist liturgical practice and uttered the celebrated dictum that he would not have as a teacher or ordained minister anyone who could not sing. Theology, said Luther, begins where music leads. Singing is a 'divine creation' by which the human being can be brought to faith, a result of the movement of the Holy Spirit, enabling the soul to 'hear, and trust, and follow'. As a consequence the Lutheran Church began by placing tremendous emphasis on the hymn chorale, on the members of the congregation singing together in their own music and in their own language.

For Australian indigenous peoples the power of the law of the Dreamtime can only be evoked by the appropriate songs. These are permanently tied to nature, to particular local waterholes, rocks, animals, plants and so on. Songs are also maps. Chester Schultz describes it thus: 'These sacred songs are said to be primordial and the authors are totemic ancestors, not human beings. The songs are handed down carefully in a system of age-graded musical education, which at all levels is a medium for religious knowledge and attitude, including history and law. In the higher reaches it is revelation, attainable only by first passing the prerequisite lower stages. To be able to sing the appropriate parts of the repertoire is essential if any child is to eventually take his or her place in society. Some of the repertoire is shared by all, but some is the protected secret of a particular group, defined by sex, clan, or stage of maturity. Songs regulate and instruct every stage of a person's life.' (*Our Place, Our Music*, 1989)

In indigenous cultures singing has long been used as a healing tool. The Australian anthropologist Diane Bell told me of an occasion when her young daughter was taken ill with food poisoning during a prolonged field trip among the Kaytej people at Warrabri in outback Australia. Because of the Kaytej women's acceptance of Bell and her daughter as kin they spontaneously began to treat the sick child as they would one born to them. Placing her in the centre of a circle they massaged her abdomen, gave her quantities of water and then sang to her for between three to four hours. The songs the Kaytej women sang were songs of that part of the country and the people who belonged to it. As Bell says in her remarkable book, *Daughters of the Dreaming* (1983) the Kaytej concept of health is a cosmic one which entails the maintenance of harmonic relations between people and place. The individual who is ill has lost his or her sense of connection. The singing is a restoration, a 'putting-in-touch-with' process. The songs of your country reconnect you; they restore you to harmony with what is around you and those to whom you belong.

Such instances were once patronisingly described as a kind of faith healing but there are many recorded instances of resolute sceptics being greatly affected by ritual singing and, in particular, ritually intoned high frequency sounding. A group of acquaintances from my university days, card-carrying rationalists and sceptics all, were invited on one occasion to attend a meeting of an Indian spiritual group where, during the evening, chanting of the usual kind was conducted for almost an hour; nothing exceptional, but what one might expect to encounter in any suburban ashram. By the end of it one of the sceptical party had dissolved into tears. Another, a young law student, visibly affected, declared that 'they' must have put some kind of gas through the air vents, thereby illustrating how easily in straining to find a rational explanation within a very limited model one can tip over into the irrational. This was not a mistake made by that most sceptical of philosophers the English positivist Herbert Spencer. Music, he wrote, is one of the few things the rational mind cannot explain: it is 'an incomprehensible secret'.

3

Not the least interesting aspect of Tomatis's conclusions is the way in which they connect up with the work of some theorists in the areas of psychology and psychoanalysis. As in the British object relations school of psychoanalysis, Tomatis placed great emphasis on the role of the mother, in his case going back even to the earliest days of the womb and the power of the mother's voice as primary sensation. More than that, Tomatis idealises the prenatal environment as a kind of nirvana. Critic Tim Wilson has characterised it as 'an auditory paradise, a condition of "super hearing" to which we aspire throughout our lives to return' (Campbell, 1996). For me there is something in this that resonates with the attempts of British art theorist, the late Peter Fuller to explain and defend the function of art.

Like Tomatis, Fuller has something of a messianic tone to his work. The atheist son of a church pastor, Fuller turned to psychoanalysis for an explanation of why artistic pursuits, like singing, might be deemed essential to the mental well-being of ordinary people. Drawing on the object relations school of psychoanalysis, especially the work of Donald Winnicott, Fuller invokes art as the 'potential space' that enables us to escape from 'the insult of the reality principle', that is, the drudgery of earning a living. On Winnicott's model, one of the effects of the human infant's prolonged infancy is that the infant begins life in a blissfully uncomplicated state. Around the time of weaning, however, the so-called reality principle begins to intrude, a realisation that the world is a harsh place that does not exist purely for the infant's own personal benefit. This transition from a world that is entirely subjective experience to one that is objectively perceived as outside the self is a painful one. The infant loses his or her sense of oneness with the world having already lost a sense of oneness with the mother in the womb. To compensate the infant establishes an intermediate area of experience between objective and subjective reality, a 'potential space' of play. In this one area, says Fuller, we are free from the insult of the reality principle. How satisfyingly we can be free of it, and for how long, depends on how nurturing our environment is and the valuation it gives to creative play in adult life.

In post-industrial times, argues Fuller, 'the aesthetic dimension has been hopelessly marginalised and the potential space, at least as the location of adult cultural experience has been effectively sealed over' (*Aesthetics after Modernism*, 1982). With industrialisation 'the potential space began to shrink. The insult of the reality principle impinged deeper and deeper into the lives of ordinary people. There was no room for an intermediate area on production lines, at the pit-head or in steel furnaces.' Art was no longer an element in man's lived relation to the world, as it had been in indigenous cultures and even in pre-industrial rural and cottage industry. The artist, says Fuller, became separate and 'special'.

On this model, singing is simply one of the many forms of artistic activity that offer us a break from the established reality principle. And indeed this is strongly echoed in something that Stephen Schafer, the Musical Director of the Sydney Gay and Lesbian Choir said in an interview he gave to Sydney writer Teresa Savage in 1996. When asked what members got out of singing in the choir, Schafer cited 'the psychology of setting time aside when you can stop worrying about the problems of day-to-day life, of living in a sad household or having a difficult job – it's time out, it's another place, it's art rather than reality. It might relate to reality very strongly but it is after all not reality as such, it's not the whole thing. It's reflective, or contemplative, interior time. Ironically, when you're all together singing, the last thing you worry about are the day-to-day stresses of being gay and lesbian.'

Micheál McCarthy, Musical Director of Sisongke, makes a similar point. 'You have to look at where singing sits in relation to the rest of our lives. For some people it's very different from what they do during the week. Some have said that it's a real high for them because their normal routine involves sitting in front of computers punching numbers, typing or drafting reports, dealing with benchmarks, competencies, daily measurement targets and the many levels of rationalisation that inhere in certain work. It's a completely different mind-set.'

Undoubtedly it is true that singers in a choir seek to immerse themselves in a subjective, a feeling moment as a way of escaping from stress, but it is also true that they wish to escape into something much more than just a space of 'discharge and release'. This they can do through jogging, or working-out in the gym. But they also seek an escape not just for its own sake, but in order to enter into a space that is powerfully charged with an experience of union. Stephen Schafer captures the inherent paradox of this when he says that singing 'sort of amplifies your self and you lose yourself in it at the same time. That's teamwork at its best. You're part of a greater whole. That sort of stuff is exhilarating; it's thrilling. It's the moment of performance itself, when you're out of time, when the song is it, when you and the choir are making something fantastic, and there's silence and you. That's the universe, that's a great moment, a moment of transcendence if you like.'

What is it that David Brennan says? 'Being in the present moment is what music is. There is no other purpose to music! It is completely evanescent. It is the ultimate Zen experience. It has no other purpose than to be in the moment, and disappear.'

Psychoanalysis might interpret this as a desire to regress to the nirvana of the womb. Social anthropologists might argue for it as an attempt to achieve a sense of community, with the choir, say, as one of many possible communities. In *Aesthetics after Modernism* Peter Fuller quotes Edmund Leach, the English social anthropologist. 'Each of us is constantly engaged, almost from birth, in a struggle to distinguish I from other, while at the same time trying to ensure that I does not become wholly isolated from other.' And this, says Leach (and Fuller), is where art comes in: 'It is the bridge we need to save ourselves from schizophrenia.' If one model of this connection that Leach refers to is the community choir then this may go some way towards explaining why the choir continues to be one of the most resilient of our social institutions.

The German philosopher Ernst Bloch believed that it was the function of music to create a utopian space where inner and outer world, subject and object, mind and nature might be reconciled beyond their present divided condition. Bloch writes of the powerful yearning for a perfected self (shades of *sacre egoism*) which behind all superficial egotism is part and parcel of a drive toward a world itself transfigured. In other words, in every narcissistic project of the so-called Me Generation is the seed of a wider Utopian field.

Bloch is just one of a long line of German philosophers (Nietzsche, Schopenhauer, Hegel) to grapple in philosophical terms with the power of music. All agree, though with greatly varying emphases, that in some fashion music enables people to enter into another dimension. One of the most influential of the modem German musicologists, Victor Zuckerkandl, is adamant on this point. Wittgenstein was wrong, he argues, to write that 'what we cannot speak of we must consign to silence'. 'Not at all,' says Zuckerkandl, 'what we cannot speak of we can sing about.' (*Man the Musician*, 1976) He goes on to postulate the reality of an additional dimension, neither inner nor outer but both at once. The singer experiences inner life as something he shares with the world, not as something that sets him apart from it. Music is a form of self-abandon, 'and this is not a turning away from the self, not a negation, but an enlargement, an enhancement of the self, a breaking down of the barriers separating self from things . . .' (Stephen Schafer: '[singing] sort of amplifies your self and you lose yourself in it at the same time.')

This is an argument that runs strongly counter to the behaviourist and utilitarian view that music's function is simply the discharge of tension, like quenching your thirst. From the opposite point of view, the most important thing about music is not that it eliminates something from the world but that it adds something to it. The more radical of the musicologists, thinkers of the school of *Musica Speculativa* such as Marius Schneider and Rudolf Haase go even further. Schneider is a distinguished ethno-musicologist with a strong spiritual bent, coiner of the term 'acoustic spirituality' which refers to the belief that the essence of the soul is not air but vibration, sound. The first postulate of speculative music is that sound (or tone, or music) is ontologically prior to material existence. In active participation in music, i.e. singing or playing, man taps into the primordial acoustic energy of creation. This is why, says Schneider, all public ritual is accompanied by music and songs, a hearkening back to archaic practices. A student of the Vedas, he quotes from the *Shatapatha Brahmana*: 'Whatever the gods do, they do by song.' Singing calls creation into being and then sustains it; in the *Rigveda* the terms food and hymn are used practically as synonyms. All songs, says Schneider, are intrinsically songs of praise in that they are about the hunger for and affirmation of life. In the Hindu scriptures, since God resides in the innermost part of every person, to sing the praise of God is to bring about the merger of the human and the divine – one brings one's own innermost nature into harmony with the word of creation from which all creatures have sprung.

In other words we move from separation into union; we are saved from schizophrenia; we embrace the singing cure.

4

Work-in-Progress

It's Tuesday night in the Trinity Hall and it's now the middle of winter and the heating has failed and I am so cold I can barely get my voice out. One of the group is organising a night at the Bruce Beresford film *Paradise Road*, about a group of women in a Japanese prisoner-of-war camp who sing in a choir all through their incarceration. 'At least they were warm,' says Beatrice, *sotto voce* and rolling her eyes in my direction. She is giving out the sheet music – lost on me since I can't read it, though my newest resolution is that I will have to learn.

When I joined this group, all I brought with me was a vague notion that there was something in my life that I needed to do that I had hitherto left undone. And, lurking in my unconscious, an apparently mundane research finding, courtesy of Aaron, that had once prompted me to a new curiosity about that part of the self that wants to sing. That 'I' clearly has a fierce desire to draw attention to itself out there in the spotlight, all eyes on me . . . ME . . . (Look, Mum, look) . . . the narcissistic self, one minute flaunting its wounds, dressing them up in the finest clothes available – 'I will now sing the aria, "*Un aura amorosa*" from Mozart's *Cosi Fan Tutti*' – disguising, titivating, camouflaging the loneliness of the long-distance ego.

Singing alone.

And then, in the group, the ensemble, that other self blooms, the one that wants to forget all that, wants to lose the very thing it thought, or at times thinks, is so precious, that ego in the spotlight; wants to become not one – a supremely refined or developed single consciousness – but One; wants to be part of something larger, some whole; wants not to shine alone but to connect, to be immersed in an oceanic consciousness. *Ecstasis:* to be taken out of.

Singing with others.

Standing here tonight, among these 'others', I don't think there is any one answer to the question of why people sing, any more than there is one answer to the question of why people read books, or garden, or why they want to have children. Winnicott's potential space is much larger and more mysterious than Fuller imagined, something Winnicott himself recognised when he declared, with humility rare in analysts, that 'the self naturally knows more than we do'. In his last work he went beyond even this to a final paradox which is an acknowledgement of some essential mystery. The self, he wrote, has an urgent need to communicate with others, but a still more urgent need, in its depths, to remain unfound. The self is elusive, the player of hide and seek. It wants to be both separate and connected, to shine alone *and* lose itself in the group.

This had crystallised for me one night here in the singing group when we were asked to break into small groups and do a vocal improvisation on our own names. Some groups took to it with relish; mine winced at the idea and made a silent protest by delivering its improvisation in mime. We were agreed on this: we didn't want to draw attention to our own attempts at wit or invention, we didn't want to have to bother with wit and invention at all; we wanted to lose ourselves in someone else's music. There were others there who put on spectacular and elaborate displays; they were gifted and urgent soloists, there to be noticed, and that was fine with me. But there were those of us who came to sing in order to be lost to sight, to be in it and at the same time out of it. Not passively and silently, but actively and in full voice, unfound.

Meanwhile I have been invited this evening to join the basses and try myself out there. For comfort. I am still having trouble with 'the mask'. There is all this empty space in the head – truly – all these resonating chambers, and I have yet to learn how to free-float in them, how to 'float the sound'. I know that once I position myself among the basses with their earthy, anchored sound I'll begin to feel restless and my ear will become attuned to Bridie and the sopranos, and I will go on singing, as I've begun, in a state of uncertainty. But that's okay. One day I'll manage to get out of my own way.

The Choral Singer (ii)

'Wherever I go, I sing. It's like: have score, will travel. When I lived in Newcastle for a while I joined a choir there. When I was in New York last year I went and sang in the public *Messiah*. It was the twelfth of

December. No rehearsal, you just went. You pay a ticket to go in, it's four dollars or something. You go there to have a hit. There are three thousand voices in the auditorium at the Lincoln Centre and whole office parties go. That's their end-of-year function, the whole office goes and sings *The Messiah*. You've got to be able to hold your part because you don't know who's around you; you've got a guy on one side singing the bass and a guy on the other singing the tenor part. Is it chaotic? Well, it's fabulously good fun because you've got to enjoy and trust your voice. You think: I'm not going to be a mouse, I came here to sing this thing. And off you go. And you just have a great time.

'When I was working in England, I sang there as well. I was living in a village called Brightwell. I'd just had a day showing my stuff for the European market and I'd had big rows with our producer over there, and he was mean and nasty and I got back to the village feeling: What on earth am I doing here? Why do I stay here? I still had another three or four months to go of my contract. And it was a miserable grey day and I just fell apart, just weeping for hours. What will I do? What will I do? And then I remembered, exactly opposite our house, Brightwell Manor, just over the road was a little old village church with lots of gravestones and big trees, and the last time I'd gone for a walk there I'd seen a notice pinned on a tree saying the choir was about to start. And I didn't know whether it was that week or the last week or the next week, but I was so miserable, and I knew that if you sing you feel better. I was thinking about how when black prisoners of conscience were taken into places of detention like Robben Island in South Africa, the other prisoners would come and take them and say: You must sing, it's the only way to stay up, you must sing. You have to sing, otherwise you'll lose your spirit. I don't know where I read this, but I remembered it. So I went over the road and the notice was still there. And it was actually that very night that the choir was starting. So I took down the phone number and ran back to the house and I rang up the guy who lived in a village nearby and I said to him, "Look, I'm an Australian, I'm only here for a few months, I won't be here for when the Christmas concert season is on but I really would like to sing and come to the choir tonight" (which was only a hundred yards up the road in The Free Church). And he said: "Well, of course." He said: "Everybody sings." And it is a tradition in England that everybody sings. Every village has a choir and it's not just a glee club, it's a proper choir with a proper choir director and you sing real pieces. And that evening we were doing *The Messiah* and a Mozart piece. It was serious music and he was a very nice choirmaster. And when I got home I just felt so much better. And I thought: it's true, you just have to sing and you get your spirit back.'

Acknowledgments

I am especially grateful to Helen Todd for her forbearance and wise counsel during the research of this book, though she can in no way be held accountable for its limitations.

I am also indebted to the generosity of the following people: Mati-Jo Beams, Diane Bell, David Brennan, Stephanie Dowrick, Beatrice Kelly, Jody Heald, Valanga Khoza, Andrew Lohrey, Brigid Lohrey, Cleo Lohrey, Stacey Loukis, Micheál McCarthy, Wayne McDaniel, Victoria Rigney, Marnie Rogers, Teresa Savage, Steven Schafer, Lyn Tranter, Jasmine Trethewey, Sarah Walker and all the members of the Tuesday night singing group.

CPSIA information can be obtained
at www.ICGtesting.com
Printed in the USA
LVHW080157270422
717354LV00011B/759

9 780987 593801